Joyce Appleby on *Thomas Jefferson*
Louis Auchincloss on *Theodore Roosevelt*
Jean H. Baker on *James Buchanan*
H. W. Brands on *Woodrow Wilson*
Douglas Brinkley on *Gerald R. Ford*
Josiah Bunting III on *Ulysses S. Grant*
James MacGregor Burns and Susan Dunn on *George Washington*
Charles W. Calhoun on *Benjamin Harrison*
Gail Collins on *William Henry Harrison*
Robert Dallek on *Harry S. Truman*
John W. Dean on *Warren G. Harding*
John Patrick Diggins on *John Adams*
E. L. Doctorow on *Abraham Lincoln*
Elizabeth Drew on *Richard M. Nixon*
Annette Gordon-Reed on *Andrew Johnson*
Henry F. Graff on *Grover Cleveland*
David Greenberg on *Calvin Coolidge*
Gary Hart on *James Monroe*
Hendrik Hertzberg on *Jimmy Carter*
Roy Jenkins on *Franklin Delano Roosevelt*
Zachary Karabell on *Chester Alan Arthur*
Lewis H. Lapham on *William Howard Taft*
William E. Leuchtenburg on *Herbert Hoover*
Timothy Naftali on *George Bush*
Kevin Phillips on *William McKinley*
Robert V. Remini on *John Quincy Adams*
Ira M. Rutkow on *James A. Garfield*
John Seigenthaler on *James K. Polk*
Hans L. Trefousse on *Rutherford B. Hayes*
Tom Wicker on *Dwight D. Eisenhower*
Ted Widmer on *Martin Van Buren*
Sean Wilentz on *Andrew Jackson*
Garry Wills on *James Madison*

James Monroe

Gary Hart

James
Monroe

THE AMERICAN PRESIDENTS

ARTHUR M. SCHLESINGER, JR., GENERAL EDITOR

Times Books

HENRY HOLT AND COMPANY, NEW YORK

Times Books
Henry Holt and Company, LLC
Publishers since 1866
175 Fifth Avenue
New York, New York 10010

Henry Holt® is a registered trademark of Henry Holt and Company, LLC.

Washington Crossing the Delaware by Emanuel Gottlieb Leutze
© Bettmann/ CORBIS
ISBN-13: 978-0-8050-6960-0
ISBN-10: 0-8050-6960-7

Printed in the United States of America

For Arthur Schlesinger, Jr.,
in appreciation of the great contributions
he has made to our nation.

Contents

Editor's Note

The president is the central player in the American political order. That would seem to contradict the intentions of the Founding Fathers. Remembering the horrid example of the British monarchy, they invented a separation of powers in order, as Justice Brandeis later put it, "to preclude the exercise of arbitrary power." Accordingly, they divided the government into three allegedly equal and coordinate branches—the executive, the legislative, and the judiciary.

But a system based on the tripartite separation of powers has an inherent tendency toward inertia and stalemate. One of the three branches must take the initiative if the system is to move. The executive branch alone is structurally capable of taking that initiative. The Founders must have sensed this when they accepted Alexander Hamilton's proposition in the Seventieth Federalist that "energy in the executive is a leading character in the definition of good government." They thus envisaged a strong president—but within an equally strong system of constitutional accountability. (The term *imperial presidency* arose in the 1970s to describe the situation when the balance between power and accountability is upset in favor of the executive.)

The American system of self-government thus comes to focus in the presidency—"the vital place of action in the system," as

Woodrow Wilson put it. Henry Adams, himself the great-grandson and grandson of presidents as well as the most brilliant of American historians, said that the American president "resembles the commander of a ship at sea. He must have a helm to grasp, a course to steer, a port to seek." The men in the White House (thus far only men, alas) in steering their chosen courses have shaped our destiny as a nation.

Biography offers an easy education in American history, rendering the past more human, more vivid, more intimate, more accessible, more connected to ourselves. Biography reminds us that presidents are not supermen. They are human beings too, worrying about decisions, attending to wives and children, juggling balls in the air, and putting on their pants one leg at a time. Indeed, as Emerson contended, "There is properly no history; only biography."

Presidents serve us as inspirations, and they also serve us as warnings. They provide bad examples as well as good. The nation, the Supreme Court has said, has "no right to expect that it will always have wise and humane rulers, sincerely attached to the principles of the Constitution. Wicked men, ambitious of power, with hatred of liberty and contempt of law, may fill the place once occupied by Washington and Lincoln."

The men in the White House express the ideals and the values, the frailties and the flaws, of the voters who send them there. It is altogether natural that we should want to know more about the virtues and the vices of the fellows we have elected to govern us. As we know more about them, we will know more about ourselves. The French political philosopher Joseph de Maistre said, "Every nation has the government it deserves."

At the start of the twenty-first century, forty-two men have made it to the Oval Office. (George W. Bush is counted our forty-third president, because Grover Cleveland, who served nonconsecutive terms, is counted twice.) Of the parade of presidents, a dozen or so lead the polls periodically conducted by historians and political scientists. What makes a great president?

Great presidents possess, or are possessed by, a vision of an ideal America. Their passion, as they grasp the helm, is to set the ship of state on the right course toward the port they seek. Great presidents also have a deep psychic connection with the needs, anxieties, dreams of people. "I do not believe," said Wilson, "that any man can lead who does not act . . . under the impulse of a profound sympathy with those whom he leads—a sympathy which is insight—an insight which is of the heart rather than of the intellect."

"All of our great presidents," said Franklin D. Roosevelt, "were leaders of thought at a time when certain ideas in the life of the nation had to be clarified." So Washington incarnated the idea of federal union, Jefferson and Jackson the idea of democracy, Lincoln union and freedom, Cleveland rugged honesty. Theodore Roosevelt and Wilson, said FDR, were both "moral leaders, each in his own way and his own time, who used the presidency as a pulpit."

To succeed, presidents not only must have a port to seek but they must convince Congress and the electorate that it is a port worth seeking. Politics in a democracy is ultimately an educational process, an adventure in persuasion and consent. Every president stands in Theodore Roosevelt's bully pulpit.

The greatest presidents in the scholars' rankings, Washington, Lincoln, and Franklin Roosevelt, were leaders who confronted and overcame the republic's greatest crises. Crisis widens presidential opportunities for bold and imaginative action. But it does not guarantee presidential greatness. The crisis of secession did not spur Buchanan or the crisis of depression spur Hoover to creative leadership. Their inadequacies in the face of crisis allowed Lincoln and the second Roosevelt to show the difference individuals make to history. Still, even in the absence of first-order crisis, forceful and persuasive presidents—Jefferson, Jackson, James K. Polk, Theodore Roosevelt, Ronald Reagan—are able to impose their own priorities on the country.

The diverse drama of the presidency offers a fascinating set of tales. Biographies of American presidents constitute a chronicle of wisdom and folly, nobility and pettiness, courage and cunning, forthrightness and deceit, quarrel and consensus. The turmoil perennially swirling around the White House illuminates the heart of the American democracy.

It is the aim of the American Presidents series to present the grand panorama of our chief executives in volumes compact enough for the busy reader, lucid enough for the student, authoritative enough for the scholar. Each volume offers a distillation of character and career. I hope that these lives will give readers some understanding of the pitfalls and potentialities of the presidency and also of the responsibilities of citizenship. Truman's famous sign—"The buck stops here"—tells only half the story. Citizens cannot escape the ultimate responsibility. It is in the voting booth, not on the presidential desk, that the buck finally stops.

—Arthur M. Schlesinger, Jr.

James Monroe

Introduction:
James Monroe, Soldier

Shifting silently through the bitter December cold like eerie por-
tents on the battlements of Elsinore, the shadowy figures set off the
dogs. They in turn roused the occupant of the house near the intersection of the Pennington road and the highway connecting Trenton
to Princeton to the north. Out he came, "violent and determined in
his manner, and very profane," according to a young revolutionary
soldier.[1] Convinced he was confronting soldiers of the British army
before dawn on this day following Christmas, the resident ordered
them off.

The young lieutenant, merely eighteen years of age, who earlier
that year had been a sophomore at the College of William and Mary,
assured the furious local that he and his men were Continentals, an
advance detachment of the Third Virginia Regiment under the command of Captain William Washington; whereupon the good, though
still sleepy, man insisted that the lieutenant and freezing platoon
come inside for food and warmth. Citing their duty to protect the
road into Trenton, the soldiers reluctantly declined. Now suddenly
alert, the resident identified himself as Dr. John Riker, brought welcome food out to the hungry soldiers, and insisted on joining them. "I
may be of some help to some poor fellow," he said, and immediately
enlisted as a surgeon-volunteer in the Continental army of America. It was about seven-thirty in the morning, December 26, 1776.

Leutze's famous painting *Washington Crossing the Delaware* shows Washington's lieutenant, the future president James Monroe, holding the American flag.

Led by General George Washington who, with an army of about 2,400 men, had just crossed the Delaware River on his flat-bottom Durham boat, the main American columns arrived shortly down the main highways from the north. Within minutes, the Continental army set upon the Hessian forces at Trenton, still abed, and fierce fighting ensued. On King Street in the center of town, the Hessians unlimbered artillery pieces aimed at the American regiments pouring down the streets from the north.

Joined by New Englanders led by Sergeant Joseph White, Captain Washington and the Third Virginians charged the guns. At the head of his troops Captain Washington attacked, ran off the enemy troops around the cannon, and took possession of them, going down with severe wounds to both hands. His lieutenant assumed command of the company and continued the assault. Very soon he took a musket ball high in the shoulder, severing an artery. But Dr. John Riker, the New Jersey physician who had volunteered only an hour or two before, clamped off the artery and saved his life.

There is no evidence to establish that the young lieutenant had occupied General Washington's barge earlier that morning, but he would be immortalized some seventy-five years later by the painter Emanuel Leutze as a determined figure placed immediately behind Washington in his painting *Washington Crossing the Delaware.* That lieutenant, made captain for his bravery at Trenton later in the day, would become the fifth president of the United States and the last veteran of the American Revolution to serve in that capacity. His name was James Monroe.

From the spring of 1776, when he was commissioned a second lieutenant in the Third Virginia Regiment at the age of seventeen, until near the close of 1781, when as a twenty-three-year-old colonel his duties ended, James Monroe was a military man. For virtually the entire first five years of his early adulthood, Monroe saw military service in the cause of the American Revolution.

Like Washington, but unlike John Adams, Thomas Jefferson, or James Madison, Monroe was a military man before he was a diplomat or politician. And like Andrew Jackson and other military veterans to follow, Monroe viewed the future of the young republic through the lens of what today we would call defense or national security. The faint but lingering smell of gunpowder would cause him to be concerned with defining the nation's southern and western boundaries and its position in the Western Hemisphere.

Monroe lacked Jefferson's eclectic didacticism and Madison's conceptual grasp of political theory. But like Washington, he knew how to mount a warrior horse, ford an icy river, and lead men in combat. If the world, or at least the Revolutionary American world, could be divided between men of thought and men of action, Monroe and his commander in chief, George Washington, were very much men of action.

Action for James Monroe began even before his lieutenant's commission. Even before the battles at Lexington and Concord, William and Mary students were organizing militia companies and conducting drills on the Palace Green in Williamsburg in full view of Lord Dunmore, the Crown's governor in the Virginia colony. Within days of Lexington and Concord and before fleeing his governor's mansion,

Dunmore had prudently ordered ashore the crew of His Majesty's ship *Magdalen* in the dead of night to empty the local powder magazine, fearing, he told the suddenly alerted townspeople, a slave uprising. This patent subterfuge, when coupled with news of the dead Massachusetts minutemen received on April 29, 1775, caused Dunmore to flee for his life within days. His departure was hastened, no doubt, by the growing number of student militia companies and frontier units, one of which was led by a young John Marshall, arriving in Williamsburg.

No record confirms James Monroe's participation in these militias, but given his early physical maturity, familiarity with military drill, and participation in a youthful band that liberated the arsenal stashed in the abandoned governor's mansion, it is difficult to imagine him in absentia from the militarized hothouse of revolutionary Williamsburg. Upon receiving his second lieutenant's commission, he was not yet eighteen, but, in the words of one biographer, "he was tall and strong, an excellent horseman and a fine shot."[2]

The Third Virginians, commanded by Colonel George Weedon of Fredericksburg, joined Washington's Continental army at Harlem Heights, north of New York City, in mid-September 1776. For Monroe's immediate commander in the regiment's seventh company, Captain William Washington, it was a reunion with his more famous distant cousin. The British under Lord Richard Howe, having landed in Manhattan at Kip's Bay (now the foot of East Thirty-fourth Street), had moved northward, and a skirmish that came to be known as the Battle of Harlem Heights ensued. It was Monroe's first experience under enemy guns.

By the end of October, Washington, whose forces were outnumbered by at least two to one, with desertions widening the odds constantly, withdrew to New Rochelle, then to White Plains, where, on the twenty-fifth, Monroe participated in a "brief, bloody battle."[3] Washington then divided his forces, and shortly thereafter the Continental detachments sent to defend Fort Washington and Fort Lee were defeated. Uncertain of Lord Howe's movements, the main body of Washington's army crossed the Hudson River to

Hackensack, New Jersey, and, closely pursued, thence to Newark. Washington's retreat continued southward to Brunswick, then to Princeton, then to Trenton, where, in early December, he had all Delaware River boats on that stretch of the river collected across from the city. On the night of December 7, as the Hessian grenadiers under the command of Colonel Johann Rall closed in, the ragged, barefoot Continentals crossed to the Pennsylvania side of the Delaware on the grab-bag riverboat flotilla.

Young Lieutenant Monroe's regiment was centrally involved in this historic strategic retreat, a retreat described by another of its participants, Thomas Paine, in this fashion:

> With a handful of men, we sustained an orderly retreat for nearly a hundred miles, brought off our ammunition, all our fieldpieces, the greatest part of our stores, and had four rivers to pass. None can say that our retreat was precipitate, for we were three weeks in performing it, that the country might have time to come.[4]

Despite the fact that the Hessians had now dug in at Trenton and waited for warmer weather to cross over and take Philadelphia, Washington recognized what he called "the perplexity of my situation" and that "no man . . . ever had a greater choice of difficulties, and less means to extricate himself from them."[5]

The means by which Washington chose to extricate himself from these difficulties was notable for its audacity and was, to some, the turning point of the Revolutionary War. He would choose Christmas night to recross the ice-choked river and attack the enemy: "Necessity, dire necessity, will, nay must, justify an attempt," he claimed by way of explanation. As each regiment mustered on that bitter Christmas night, Washington had read to them Thomas Paine's exhortation written (in words reminiscent of Shakespeare's Henry V) days before: "These are the times that try men's souls. The summer soldier and the sunshine patriot will, in this crisis, shrink from the service of his country. But he that stands it now deserves the love and thanks of man and woman." Early the next morning as they poised before the sleeping city of Trenton, the watchword was "Victory or death."

James Monroe's regiment was among the first to cross the Delaware on December 26. Captain William Washington's company was quickly dispatched, between three and four in the sleet-driven morning, southward from the ford at McKinley's Ferry to seal off the intersection of the Pennington and Lawrenceville roads north of Trenton against any early morning traveler inclined to alert the slumbering Hessians. When artillery pieces were finally off-loaded from the Durham boats, two columns, one under General John Sullivan, down the River road, and another under General Nathanael Greene, down the Pennington road (including an artillery battery under Captain Alexander Hamilton), moved on Trenton shortly after dawn.

Sullivan's cannon were the first to open up. Hessians poured from their barracks and manned two brass three-pound guns pointed up King Street at William Washington's rapidly advancing company. It was in this action that Washington's hands were badly injured in the successful and necessary assault on the guns and Lieutenant Monroe took the musket ball to the shoulder that could have ended his life had the severed artery not been tied off by his new patriot friend Dr. Riker. Made captain by George Washington for his bravery, and after two months' recuperation, the eighteen-year-old Monroe returned to Virginia on a recruitment trip to raise more troops for the Continental army.

By August 1777, with no company of his own to command, Captain Monroe returned to the Continental army and became an aide to Lord Stirling (Major General William Alexander), a colorful soldier with an ancient Scottish title. Monroe saw action at Brandywine Creek on September 11, where he tended to a wounded Marquis de Lafayette—who became a lifelong friend—and participated in a failed surprise attack on British forces at Germantown on October 4. Though Monroe does not appear in dispatches from subsequent battles around Philadelphia for control of the Delaware, by November 20 he had been promoted to major and made Stirling's official aide-de-camp.

The historic, miserable, and courageous winter at Valley Forge ensued. The winter and its misery were finally lifted in March 1778 by the announcement of an alliance with France. Then, in mid-June, with the British evacuation of Philadelphia and Washington's pursuit, once again across the Delaware northward into New Jersey, Major Monroe reported to General Washington that he was within four hundred yards of the British encampment at Monmouth Court House with seventy fatigued men: "If I had six horsemen I think If I co'd serve you in no other way I sho'd in the course of the night procure good intelligence." Appointed adjutant general to Stirling during the battle at Monmouth, Monroe helped repel the British attack on his division.

Monroe continued to serve under Washington through the summer and fall of 1778, as his army moved back up to White Plains, New York, near where Monroe had first joined up. After spending the winter in Philadelphia and possibly strapped by his self-financed service, Monroe made his way back to Virginia. In the spring of 1779, Monroe received a commission as lieutenant colonel from the Virginia Assembly, but once again the assembly did not have sufficient revenues to raise a militia regiment for him to command. Instead, he was appointed aide to Governor Thomas Jefferson while he began his study of the law. Then in June 1780, he was appointed military commissioner by Governor Jefferson's council with the mandate to establish a communications link between Baron de Kalb's southern army, which was facing Cornwallis and Tarleton in North Carolina, and the government of Virginia, thus making Monroe an early military intelligence officer.

By late 1780, Virginia itself had come under attack from advancing British forces and Monroe, now made a colonel, commanded an "emergency regiment," though it seems to have contributed little to the defense of the Old Dominion. Monroe continued to lobby in various quarters for further militia commands, largely to no avail. With Cornwallis's surrender at Yorktown, in November 1781,

Colonel James Monroe, now twenty-three years of age, attended a
Peace Ball at Fredericksburg together with senior military officers
from the Continental army. Thus officially ended his almost six-
year military career.

When Colonel Monroe had departed George Washington's army
in White Plains on May 30, 1779, Washington addressed a letter
concerning Monroe to an associate in Virginia. "I take occasion to
express to you the high opinion I have of his worth," he wrote. "He
has, in every instance, maintained the reputation of a brave, active,
and sensible officer. [I]t were to be wished that the State [Virginia]
could do something for him, to enable him to follow the bent of his
military inclination, and render service to his country."[6]

Admittedly, assessing James Monroe through the prism of his formative military experience and consistent concern for the security
of the nation is contrary to convention. For the traditional thumb-
nail sketch of Monroe comes to something like this: he was the last
of the Virginia dynasty, less colorful and probably less intelligent
than his predecessors, and he promulgated the Monroe Doctrine
(which, the conventional wisdom holds, was really the invention of
his secretary of state, John Quincy Adams).

This assessment takes a different course. It seeks, above all, to
provide a broader view of the man, especially as patriot and public
servant. It explores Monroe's relationships with three of the dominant figures in his life, George Washington, Thomas Jefferson, and
James Madison, all Virginians and all predecessors in the presidency, and suggests that through his diplomatic service to each he
was a much stronger and more independent figure than is generally
recognized. It also considers the key relationship between Monroe
and his secretary of state, John Quincy Adams, especially to determine who actually was the dominant figure. This account positions
Monroe as the first "national security" president, whose consistent
underlying motivation was to expand and establish the borders of
the United States and to make it the dominant power in the Western Hemisphere, free of European interference. In this connection,

there is a detailed discussion of the circumstances leading up to the announcement of the Principles of 1823, later known as the Monroe Doctrine.

By the end of the narrative, it is hoped that readers will have a better understanding of James Monroe—as a more complicated, more nuanced figure than the one traditionally depicted in history books.

1

The Portrait of a Patriot

The tall, rough-hewn eighteen-year-old, quick to join his William and Mary classmates in insurrection against the king, was a product of Westmoreland County, what was called the Northern Neck of Virginia. Born on April 28, 1758, James Monroe was the son of Spence Monroe, who signed himself both carpenter and gentleman, and the former Elizabeth Jones, daughter of the architect James Jones. In 1766, when James was eight, Spence Monroe joined Northern Neck farmers in signing a pledge against the consumption of English imports until repeal of the hated Stamp Act, marking him a "patriot." James's uncle, Joseph Jones, was a judge and member of the Virginia House of Burgesses, serving on its committees that drafted the Virginia Declaration of Rights and the Virginia Constitution, and a member of the Continental Congress. Judge Jones claimed a "confidential" friendship with George Washington and close relations with both Thomas Jefferson and James Madison, and he was to be the formative early political influence on James Monroe's life, his patron, and a constant adviser on matters ranging from personal finance to high political ambition.

One biographer has written that Monroe, as an adult, "resembled his uncle in many ways—reflective, never rushing to conclusions but forming opinions deliberately. The same tact, warmth, and patience in human relations, so pronounced in the judge's character, were equally apparent in the nephew."[1] Later in life, when it came to confrontation with Alexander Hamilton, Edmund Randolph, less directly John Adams, and even George Washington himself, Monroe's tact and patience would be sorely tested and frayed.

Young Monroe was accompanied on his long, woods-lined walks to Parson Campbell's school, Campbelltown Academy, by his neighbor and friend John Marshall, the future chief justice of the United States. With their schoolbooks in mathematics and Latin, both boys carried frontier rifles. Marshall, slightly older, would also join Monroe at William and Mary in 1774 and from there into the Continental army. Just three months after the Revolutionary Virginia Convention passed its own "declaration of independence" on May 15, 1776, Lieutenant Monroe, with the Third Virginia Regiment, marched out of Williamsburg northward to join the Continentals under Washington at New York. Three years later, when Monroe headed back to Virginia seeking recruits for another regiment, he left with the letter from Washington describing his combat service in considerable detail and recommending him as "a brave, active, and sensible officer" and expressing "the high opinion I have of his worth."

Despite his plan, conveyed to Jefferson in the fall of 1781 at the conclusion of five years' military service, to travel to Europe to study, Monroe was elected to the Virginia Assembly from neighboring King George County the following year. During this period, Jefferson began his lifelong role as mentor to Monroe. "Jefferson, as he was to do on many subsequent occasions, exerted a decisive influence on Monroe's life," writes Monroe's biographer Harry Ammon. "At this time, Monroe, who was floundering about and had no idea what to do with himself, badly needed advice and encouragement. The Governor [Jefferson] provided exactly the right tonic, administered with tact, understanding, and a very real concern about the young man's fate."[2] With his friend Marshall, Monroe was soon elected to Virginia's eight-member Executive Council, "rather young for a Councillor," according to one observer. He continued on the political fast track by being elected to the fourth Confederation

Congress in June 1783 and two subsequent congresses thereafter. Rembrandt Peale's famous painting of Washington resigning his commission before the Congress in Annapolis on July 27, 1783, following the signing of a treaty of peace with England, has both Monroe and Madison foremost wearing cocked hats. Monroe, still only twenty-five, dined regularly with Jefferson before the senior figure left for France, as the American minister in Paris.

Among political leaders during this period, Monroe was on the forefront of those who viewed things nationally, rather than merely as citizens of individual states. Early on, he demonstrated the national security prism through which he was to view great events with these words regarding the many issues facing the new nation: "There are before us some questions of the utmost consequence that can arise in the councils of any nation," among them, "whether we are to have regular or standing troops to protect our frontiers, or leave them unguarded; whether we will expose ourselves to the inconveniences, which may perhaps be the loss of the country westward, from the impossibility of preventing the adventurers [pioneers] from settling where they please; the intrusion of the settlers on the European powers who border us, a cause of discontent and perhaps war."3

Here we see, presciently, Monroe's very early anticipation of matters that would dominate his own presidency decades later, the frictions caused by the new nation's natural expansion against and eventually onto the territory claimed by European powers and perhaps even the role of those powers in the entire American hemisphere. And, significantly, Monroe anticipated matters in terms ("discontent and perhaps war") of a military officer. "From the beginning," writes his biographer W. P. Cresson, "James Monroe, a former militia man, who had served beneath the Rattlesnake Flag with the pioneers, was by instinct and sympathy a 'Man of the Western Waters.' From the frontiersmen he was to draw much of his political strength and, in return, was to serve them with all the ability and energy at his command."4

Monroe's view was, at least in part, influenced by his uncle Judge

Jones, who was an early exponent of the cession of frontier lands to the federal government for the purpose of creating new states. Other proponents of this plan included Washington, Jefferson, George Mason, and others of the "new states" persuasion. For himself and others, Washington advocated reward of the frontier lands to poorly compensated Continental army veterans, a movement soon to be led by the newly formed Society of the Cincinnati. Monroe's commitment to this cause is demonstrated by his trip in the fall of 1784 through the territories west of New York and southward through the Ohio Territory, where he reported, "It is possible I may lose my scalp from the temper of the Indians, but if either a little fighting or a great deal of running will save it I shall escape safe."[5] In this, he later wrote Jefferson, he was not being entirely frivolous, for three members of his expeditions were in fact killed by angry Indians.

Monroe's interests in questions of western expansion were to preoccupy him throughout his public life. Following this early trip, he argued in the Confederation Congress for rigorous steps to garrison the former British posts on the western frontier with American troops, and he took up the emerging cause of American rights to navigate the Mississippi River. As Cresson notes:

> In the struggle for this greater empire, which now forms the might and glory of the Republic, no statesman of his time played a more significant part than James Monroe. As the champion in Congress of the still-undefined rights of the United States to the lands ceded by the Treaty of 1783 and to the free navigation of the Mississippi, he performed a service for which credit has too often been denied him. When Jefferson left for France, it was Monroe who took his place as the champion of the "Men of the Western Waters." His authority in these matters was recognized by his contemporaries and they elected him to the chairmanship of the two important committees chiefly concerned with western interests.[6]

In these matters Monroe quickly found himself at odds with John Jay, who had just been named the Confederation Congress's minister for foreign affairs. Jay was willing to sacrifice westward expansion by pioneers and frontiersmen in favor of transatlantic trading relationships with Great Britain and France on behalf of eastern commercial interests.

Jay was a New Yorker and on the side of New England and the eastern states. Their economic future was tied to the transatlantic and West Indies trade. As the dominant southern power, Virginia, together with North Carolina, claimed land west to the Mississippi and northwestward to include the Northwest Territory (today's Ohio, Michigan, Illinois, Indiana, and Wisconsin). Jefferson, who proposed ceding these claims to the national government for westward expansion, left to serve as minister to France in 1785, and Monroe took up this cause. In 1787 he succeeded in creating a territorial government through passage of the Northwest Ordinance. Jay, speaking for the eastern commercial interests, saw westward expansion and the opening of western waterways, particularly the Mississippi River and the port of New Orleans, as competition for New England. In negotiating with Spanish envoy Don Diego de Enrique Gardoqui, Jay, against his instructions, implicitly traded western interests in opening the Mississippi for expanded trade between New England and Spain.

In a letter to Patrick Henry, then governor of Virginia, on August 12, 1786, the outraged Monroe described Jay's dishonesty and manipulations: "This is one of the most extraordinary transactions I have ever known, a minister negotiating expressly for the purpose of defeating the object of his instructions, and by a long train of intrigue & management seducing the representative of the states to concur in it." He went on to summarize Jay's true intentions as "a dismemberment of the States east of the Hudson from the Union & the erection of them into a separate govt."[7] Thus the Monroe-Jay feud, to surface mightily with the Jay Treaty in 1794, was born.

During the same period Monroe's relationship with James Madison, seven years his senior, whom he had replaced in the Virginia Assembly in 1783, began to develop, largely at the initial instigation of Jefferson, who glowingly introduced him to Madison: "The scrupulousness of his honor will make you safe in the most confidential communications. A better man cannot be."[8]

Madison shared Monroe's concerns about Jay's promotion of the eastern trade interests at the expense of the frontiersmen's rights of Mississippi navigation. Monroe believed "the whole development of the Union was at stake" on this issue; upon it would depend "whether the United States was to constitute a nation or was to repeat, upon a new continent, the petty and complicated state system of Europe."[9] Like western expansion generally, the rights to navigation of the Mississippi specifically would be an issue consuming Monroe throughout most of his public life. "Indeed, until a generation of native western leaders emerged just before the War of 1812," according to one historian, "Monroe was looked upon as the only national figure identified with the aims of the West."[10]

Also during this period Monroe, who had yet to travel abroad, began to take a keen interest in foreign affairs and the appointment of appropriate diplomatic emissaries to important posts.

Two recurring themes now permeated Monroe's private life: his physical health and his financial health. Though constitutionally sturdy, he began to be plagued by a variety of ailments, some of which would send him to bed. Also, having gone virtually directly from military service into politics, he now found himself well into his twenties without a profession or a dependable source of income. Unlike his friend John Marshall, he continued to put off applying to the bar. Although described at the time as merely "respectable looking," Monroe managed to win the hand of a beautiful New York socialite, Elizabeth Kortright, who "had the hauteur of the born aristocrat and was something of a grande dame even in her girlhood," and they were married in February 1786. Later that fall Monroe resigned from Congress and, with his bride, returned to live at Judge Jones's house in Fredericksburg, where he was finally admitted to the bar.

It was a good match. Monroe's biographer Ammon summarized it thus: "The bond which united the Monroes was a remarkably close one, rendering every separation painful."[11] Jefferson took the occasion to write a letter to Monroe, meant also for his wife's eyes, regarding the glories of quiet domestic life, possibly in preference to the social whirl she had left in New York: "Quiet retirement . . . is the only point upon which the mind can settle at rest. . . . But I must not philosophize too much with her lest I give her too serious apprehensions of a friendship I shall impose upon her."[12]

Politics, however, was still very much in Monroe's blood, and within months he managed to get himself elected to the town council in Fredericksburg and soon thereafter returned to the Virginia Assembly. The first of three children—two daughters and a son who died young—was added to his new family in December 1786. But to Jefferson, who was fifteen years older than Monroe and, like Madison, now a continuous correspondent, he wrote, "My anxiety however for the gen'l welfare hath not diminished." Of these three men, whose lives were to continue to intersect for another forty or more years, one historian has written: "No personal relationship founded on common interests, opinions, and loyalties such as united these three men . . . has ever more profoundly affected the political life of a nation."[13]

In September 1787 the Constitutional Convention completed its labors, but without the participation of James Monroe. When Virginia governor Edmund Randolph had passed him over as a delegate, Monroe initially held Randolph and Madison responsible, but later he took the slight less personally. However, he did manage to become a delegate to the Virginia ratification convention in June 1788, and, as a neutral figure leaning toward the new national government and ratification—then tilting against, at least until the eloquent Madison spoke—he argued the case for the inclusion of some requirement of the federal government to guarantee his continuing cause, free navigation of the Mississippi by American frontiersmen.

Harry Ammon points out as well that Monroe "was almost alone among the anti-federalists in recommending that the federal government be given direct control over the militia as a means of eliminating the need for a standing army."[14] This was a crucial issue for both federalists and antifederalists. How could the new nation be secure from foreign threats, of which there were considerable, if defended primarily by citizen-soldiers, often not properly trained or equipped? Here Monroe's military service informed his judgment on national security matters. But he broke ranks with his republican allies adroitly. He wished the federal executive to have, under threat, the authority to "nationalize" the militia (later the National Guard) in the interest of national security—essentially the constitutional position that was to evolve many decades later.[15] James Monroe was among the first of the early national leaders to appreciate the degree to which the security of the nation had to be a responsibility of the national authority and not dependent on the individual states.

Though Monroe joined the antifederalists in voting against ratification of the proposed Constitution, he was—particularly under the influence of George Washington—among the first to cross the aisle to accept its adoption. Patrick Henry devised a gerrymandered scheme that would send a completely antifederalist delegation from Virginia to the first federal Congress, but Madison, standing in competition with Monroe for the same seat, prevailed against both. There was a major substantive disagreement between them on ratification of the Constitution: Madison thought that it should be adopted as proposed; Monroe, that it should not be ratified without amendments, including a Bill of Rights. Monroe's motives in this contest were not personal; neither resentment of Madison nor ambition for himself came into play. As Ammon observes, "Throughout his career Monroe cherished an intense, self-sacrificing acceptance of his obligations of public service, and no argument [by his supporters] was so effective in enlisting his aid as that stressing the needs of the public. . . . Monroe clearly felt that refusal to run against Madison would seem to be a betrayal of a public trust in order to gratify private friendship."[16] For Monroe, duty to country and conscience trumped personal relationships, but he never held his sense of duty to be antithetical to them. "The election over," writes Ammon, "the two friends resumed their correspondence, writing freely about politics and rendering friendly services for each other."[17]

Around Christmas 1789, Jefferson returned from his mission as minister to France to take up his post as America's first secretary of state and found his protégé James Monroe—now thirty-one years old, married, and a serious political leader in Virginia—a much more mature and self-possessed figure than the young man he had left. As Harry Ammon notes:

> The promise Jefferson had seen in [Monroe] a decade ear-
> lier had been fully realized. Yet the change was more in exter-
> nals than an inward one, for Monroe had retained all those
> qualities of warmth, sincerity and kindness which had led Jef-
> ferson to value his friendship. These attributes were now
> enriched by a mature judgment based on an extensive knowl-
> edge of public affairs. Monroe was not merely esteemed [as a]
> member of Jefferson's social circle but as a colleague whose
> views merited serious consideration. Thus the association
> between them underwent a change—Monroe was no longer a
> protégé but a coworker dedicated to the same goals as his
> friend.[18]

Monroe had become a full member in the Virginia republican tri-umvirate.

Monroe at this time undertook a personal project which had preoccupied him for some time, his relocation to Albemarle County, first to Charlottesville, then years later to property adjoin-ing Monticello. Having relocated his family and his estate to his original home in Albemarle, Monroe once again grew restless in pri-vate life. Writing to Jefferson in October 1790, he said, "I have at length yielded to my inclinations to suffer my name to be men-tion'd for a publick appointment," and in December, Monroe, now thirty-two years old, became a U.S. senator from Virginia, joining

Madison (then serving as a member of the House of Representatives) in Philadelphia, the temporary capital. His decision to accept this office was affected by an important personal consideration: living in Philadelphia would provide Mrs. Monroe proximity to her family in New York for the first time since her marriage.[19] At their request Monroe lodged with his fellow Virginians Jefferson and Madison upon his arrival in the city. One of Monroe's first acts in the Senate was to propose that the "doors of the Senate Chamber remain open" during its sessions. In his only preserved Senate speech, Monroe said: "Let the jealous, the prying eye of their constituents uphold [observe] their proceedings, mark their conduct, and the tone of the body will be changed. Many a person whose heart was devoted and whose mind pursued with unceasing ardor the establishment of arbitrary power: whilst he supposed his movements were unseen . . . wod. change his style and from motives of private interest become the fervent patron of the publick liberty."[20] He proved unpersuasive, and the doors remained closed until February 1794.

The young U.S. government soon found itself, largely under the influence of Secretary of the Treasury Alexander Hamilton and the emerging Federalist faction, engaged in a perpetual struggle over national versus states rights. The initial contest over chartering the Bank of the United States and over federal assumption of state war debts brought the combatants to the surface. Monroe was one of five senators to vote against the bank. Seeing Federalist interests becoming extensively organized, anti-Federalists began to counter this trend by organizing their own colleagues dedicated to the Republican cause. Jefferson was at the forefront, but his friends Madison and soon Monroe were enlisted as prime lieutenants. For the Federalists, the Republicans were unruly, parochial primitives. For the Republicans, the Federalists were quite simply "monarchists." A blizzard of highly partisan press columns and invective-infested pamphleteering quickly emerged on both sides. Jefferson was stage manager; Madison was chief theorist; and Monroe was organizer and foot soldier.

To compound bad feelings, in 1792 Monroe joined two other members of Congress inquiring informally into the details of the infamous Reynolds affair, in which his former comrade in arms Alexander Hamilton had become enmeshed. Hamilton's detractors had accused him of conspiring with James Reynolds in illegal monetary transactions; Hamilton confessed that he had made extortion payments to Reynolds because Reynolds's wife had been his mistress. To a degree, Hamilton held Monroe personally responsible for his humiliation, at least as an agent for Jefferson, and a breach was opened between the two that almost resulted in a resort to pistols and that was to last until Hamilton's death in his duel with Aaron Burr in 1804.

To a degree the early Federalist-Republican divisions reflected divergent regional and sectional interests. But they also were rooted in deep differences over cultural, historical, and philosophical outlooks. The Republicans, led by Virginia, were in large part the products of "the self-sufficient English manor-house system," dependent on the land, suspicious of cities, concentrated finance, and centralized government, and heavily influenced philosophically by the classic Greek and Roman republican writers.[21] By and large Federalists were shopkeepers, tradesmen, and artisans living in towns and cities, dependent on sea-based commerce, comfortable with banks and lending required by complex financing, more accepting of concentrated merchant wealth, and less suspicious of centralized government. Battle lines formed early and influenced most public policy debate, at least until the demise of the Federalist party at the end of the second decade of the nineteenth century.

Monroe's emergence as a leader of the Republican faction in the Senate led to his involvement in matters of foreign relations, then to the beginning of an almost seven-year diplomatic career abroad, which would in time lead to his appointment as secretary of state, and from that stepping-stone to the presidency. And it was in his capacity as a Senate Republican leader that Monroe was most visible in opposition to the proposed appointment in 1794 of Alexander Hamilton as minister to England. That opposition in turn led to his emergence as an identifiable friend of France and an admirer of its revolution. Monroe had already taken up the cudgel for the French revolutionaries in a series of essays written over the signature "Aratus" in 1791. In both the American and French revolutions, Monroe argued, "the power which belonged to the body of the people . . . was resumed. It now rests where it should be. . . . Whoever owns the principles of one revolution must cherish those of the other; and the person who draws a distinction between them [e.g., Hamilton] is either blinded by prejudice, or boldly denies what at the bar of reason he cannot refute."[22]

Throughout 1792 and 1793, Monroe worked closely with Jefferson and other Republicans to respond to Hamilton's accusations that Jefferson was undermining the Washington administration, that he was hostile to the Constitution, and that his pro-France leanings were undermining the interests of the new nation. Hamilton made these accusations in pamphlets he circulated over the name "Catullus." In response to the pamphlets and other accusations, Monroe and Madison produced their own series of essays, published in a Philadelphia newspaper, titled "Vindication of Mr. Jefferson." Most of the series of six pieces were written by Monroe and were sharply worded refutations of Hamilton. These contributed to Monroe's further emergence as a leading party figure and made him more visible in national circles. Before moving onto center stage, however, Monroe would require experience beyond U.S. borders in the wider world of international diplomacy. In 1794, President Washington would provide that opportunity.

By the age of thirty-eight, James Monroe had compiled a solid record of military service, had been a member of the Virginia Assembly and the Governor's Council, had served in the Confederation Congress in Annapolis, had successfully proposed the Northwest Ordinance, had participated in the constitutional ratification debates, and had been elected U.S. senator from Virginia. He had also become a member of the Virginia triumvirate, with Jefferson and Madison, of future presidents and had emerged as a leader of the informal party of Republicans. Most important, Monroe was also the leading champion of western expansion, a position that would require intense concentration on the need to secure America's southern and northern borders and expand its borders to the west. To this lifelong effort he brought the focus and intensity of mission of a combat veteran and military officer.

But it would be his service in his country's diplomatic corps that would elevate Monroe from an emerging figure in Virginia politics and Republican leader in the Senate to a serious national and international personage sufficiently experienced in foreign and domestic affairs to qualify for eventual national leadership. His first experience would be as minister to France beginning in the fall of 1794, and, after more than two years in that post during a dramatic time in U.S., British, and French relations, it would not be judged a success.

2

Washington's Lieutenant, Jefferson's Puppet, or Madison's Pawn?

The three public figures who had the most impact on James Monroe, the political figure, were George Washington, whom Monroe served as military officer and diplomatic emissary, and Thomas Jefferson and James Madison, fellow Virginians, mentors, and, in the case of Madison, occasional competitors. Popular wisdom has Monroe as the last of the "Virginia dynasty," a diminished successor to the more illustrious Jefferson and Madison. The American historian Joyce Appleby offers a more nuanced interpretation of the tiered relationships: "After his two terms, Jefferson had the exceptional good fortune to see his policies continued by two close friends, James Madison and James Monroe. This 'Virginia dynasty' lasted a quarter of a century, long enough to embed Jeffersonian values in American institutions for the entire antebellum period. The Virginia presidents imbued their successors with their understanding of the proper relation between federal and state authority, an understanding that lasted until the question of slavery rent the union and opened Americans to a new exercise of federal power."[1]

Despite uneven two-term presidencies, Jefferson and Madison cast long shadows. Jefferson—the dazzling polymath, prolific wordsmith, drafter of the Declaration of Independence, and founder of the party of Republicans. Madison—the composer of the U.S.

Constitution, genius political theorist, polemicist of *The Federalist*. Both set high standards, especially for a less gifted friend and ally. But due perhaps in part to his legal training with George Wythe, Monroe was not without some acquaintance with the classics. During the constitutional ratification process, he argued against the notion that the failure of the Amphictyonic League of Greek city-states in the fifth and fourth centuries B.C. demonstrated the inevitable weakness of federal systems, pointing out that the league was composed of city-states with mixed governments while the proposed American federation was to be composed of equal republics.[2]

The standards set by his fellow Virginia Republicans and presidents might intimidate a less stalwart figure than Monroe into quiescence and gentleman-farmer retirement. Monroe was self-reflective enough to appreciate their genius and his own comparatively commonplace talents, but not enough to be forced to the sidelines in the political combat of the day. Instead, in virtually all the dramas of national self-definition of the late eighteenth and early nineteenth centuries, Monroe moved himself, or with the help of his mentors was moved, front and center. There is little evidence that he saw himself too ordinary to participate as an equal in the struggles of the new nation at home and abroad.

Much of what we know of James Monroe the man and politician we know through his communications, service, and relationships with the three towering figures of Washington, Jefferson, and Madison. With Washington, Monroe had a complex relationship that would not conclude particularly well. With Jefferson, Monroe was deferential and solicitous and seemed genuinely to require Jefferson's guidance and approval. With Madison, Monroe assumed the role of friend and equal, sometimes soliciting advice and sometimes assuming a competitive stance. Their friendship and political alliance were not always steady.

An examination of Monroe's service with each of these historic figures offers insights into how their respective influences shaped Monroe the president. There is no evidence that Monroe, in his early military years, harbored anything but the highest esteem for his commander in chief. Though he was surely visible to Washington, even as a young officer, for his bravery and battlefield conduct, there seems to be little evidence that Washington singled him out for special notice or position as he had, for example, the young Alexander Hamilton. Toward Washington, Monroe was deferential, as befit his rank and station, without, on the other hand, being particularly reverential.

As years passed, and as Monroe rose through the political ranks to a position in the new U.S. Senate, he began to demonstrate independence from Washington as president. A particular incident is instructive. Having risen to a position of leadership among Republicans in the Senate, Monroe took it upon himself in April 1794 to object in writing to Washington to reports that the president might appoint Alexander Hamilton minister to Great Britain, and he requested an audience to make his arguments in person. "I should deem such a measure not only injurious to the publick interest, but also especially so to your own," Monroe wrote to Washington, venturing to lecture the president on his own interests regarding a man who had served under him in the Revolutionary War.[3] Washington's response to his former subordinate officer was cool, to say the least. He invited Monroe to provide any disqualifying evidence against Hamilton in writing, brushed aside his request for a personal hearing, and reminded Monroe that the appointment was his to make: "I alone am responsible for a proper nomination." Undeterred, Monroe wrote back saying that the appointment of Hamilton, an admirer of Britain and its monarchical government, would send all the wrong signals at home and abroad and would "furnish an opportunity for political intrigue against republicanism here and against our connection with France and deprive the United States of the support of a friendly power."[4] Having already decided not to pursue an appointment for Hamilton, Washington did not deign to reply. Whatever else it demonstrates, this incident clearly shows Monroe's respectful distance from and refusal to be intimidated by the iconic leader. It also illustrates the strongly partisan Republican base from which Monroe was to operate most of his life. But his streak of independence, and strong partisan Republican zeal, did not eliminate Monroe from consideration by Washington for important duties abroad shortly thereafter.

The best prism through which to view Monroe's mature relationship with Washington is through Monroe's service as Washington's emissary to France, viewed against a complicated domestic and international backdrop.

During Washington's second term in the presidency, the national government was principally concerned with the management of its relations with Great Britain and France, with Spain a close third. All were trading partners, the first two the most important ones, but all three had territorial interests on the North American continent. Britain, its recent colonial master, remained the United States' northern neighbor. France claimed a vast territory to the west of the sixteen states. And Spain held the Floridas, extending west to the British claims at New Orleans. Collectively, these three European powers defined the United States' land borders and proscribed any territorial expansion.

Matters were complicated further by the complex relations among the three European powers. Great Britain's power was on the rise, and its empire had another century to expand. France, too, was expanding its reach and, even more important, had just undergone its own revolution. Indeed, a great war between Great Britain and Napoleonic France was not too far over the horizon. Though fading in its relative powers, Spain had been for some time a colonial power in the Caribbean and in America's Southern Hemisphere.

If the young American republic was to get on in the world, it had to define and stabilize its relations with all three. And if it hoped to realize the destiny envisioned by a number of its founders, the United States had to establish its security by acquiring the Florida territory and expanding to the west. The United States negotiated its way through this complex minefield with a number of political handicaps, not least of which was its lack of credible military

authority. Republicans generally viewed a standing army as a threat
to republican government and to the concept of freedom. And it
took the Barbary pirates and the British embargo of U.S. trade with
the French West Indies before the American government would
order in 1794 the keels laid for four forty-four-gun ships and two
thirty-six-gun vessels that would become the backbone of the new
U.S. Navy.[5] Power projection, even on its own continent, was not
yet an arrow in the United States' national quiver.

Added to all this, and making the diplomatic challenge even
greater, was the emergence of the dreaded political "factions," so
feared by Jefferson among others. These factions, the forerunners of
today's political parties, domestically mirrored the principal global
struggle, that between Great Britain and France. The Federalists, the
party of Hamilton principally, but also of John Adams and many
leaders from the North, generally considered a close relationship
with Great Britain, even at the expense of good relations with
France, to be paramount. The Republicans, the party of Jefferson
principally, but also of Madison, Monroe, and most Virginians, felt a
natural affinity toward revolutionary France and its new, consider-
ably more radical, republican regime. For his part, the president
sought to stay above the fray. "Washington resisted the tug of
domestic politics not only from wishful thinking, but from policy,"
according to his biographer Richard Brookhiser. "His wishes flowed
from his policy. American passions, homegrown and imported,
might well have swept the country apart. If Washington had par-
taken of them, they certainly would have."[6]

The closer the United States moved toward Great Britain, the
more Republicans saw the betrayal of the American Revolution.
The closer the United States moved toward revolutionary France,
the more Federalists feared revolutionary, chaotic violence spread-
ing across the Atlantic to America. Having secured the nation's
independence from Great Britain, the Federalists felt no further
antipathy toward the British monarchy and sought amicable relations with their mother country. For their part, the Republicans
pursued principles antithetical to monarchy and saw closer ties to

Great Britain as antirepublican and as heralding, in the words of one historian, "the destruction of representative government in America."[7] Federalists wanted only independence from Great Britain. Republicans wanted a revolutionary new form of government incompatible with monarchy. Any American entering the diplomatic arena during the closing years of the eighteenth century undertook a perilous passage at home and abroad.

Especially in this charged climate in 1794, James Monroe was anything but a seasoned diplomat. He had served as a U.S. senator from Virginia since 1790 and was learning the new complexities of national politics. His mentor, Thomas Jefferson, was Washington's secretary of state and his colleague James Madison was speaker of the House of Representatives. As the historian Noble Cunningham has observed: "In the early leadership of a Republican party forming around Madison in the Congress and coalescing behind Jefferson in the cabinet in opposition to Hamilton, Monroe would play a similar role in the Senate as an organizer of a republican bloc."[8]

According to Cunningham, "Politics was a consuming interest for Monroe. More than either Madison or Jefferson, he was a pragmatic politician highly sensitive to contemporary currents. Monroe's letters to Jefferson and Madison dealt largely with the world of political action, not with abstract speculation. Monroe's major biographer has found that, in all the letters exchanged between Monroe and Jefferson over four decades, none dealt exclusively or at any length with philosophical or scientific pursuits, in contrast to the correspondence between Madison and Jefferson, in which philosophical discussions frequently merged with practical politics."[9]

In May 1794, France requested the recall of the American minister, Gouverneur Morris, who had made little effort to conceal his antipathy toward its radical revolution. President Washington offered the ministerial post to Robert Livingston and then to James Madison, both of whom demurred. Washington then turned to James Monroe, an avowed supporter of the French Revolution. Monroe, like all Republicans, believed that good relations with France could be achieved only by a member of their own party.[10]

Indeed, Jefferson would later describe this ambassadorial posting as one "which the public good requires to be filled by a Republican."[11] Monroe's decision to accept the appointment was also influenced by Madison, to whom he had written, "If it has not the approbation of my few friends & yourself in particular, I certainly will decline it."[12] But, in accepting the appointment, Monroe took a substantial risk, one that quite possibly could have ruined his political career.[13]

The new minister's official instructions were nuanced. President Washington wished to be known as "an early and decided friend of the French Revolution" and "immutable in his wishes for its accomplishment." Monroe was told to "show our confidence in the French Republic" and to "let it be seen, that in case of war, with any nation on earth, we shall consider France as our first and natural ally." The instructions then focused on John Jay's concurrent mission to Great Britain as it might affect the United States' relations with France. "You may say," Monroe was told, "that he [Jay] is positively forbidden to weaken the engagements between this country and France. It is not improbable that you will be obliged to encounter . . . suspicions of various kinds. But you may declare the motives of that mission to be, to obtain immediate compensation for plundered property, and restitution of the posts."[14] Whether this represented disingenuousness on Washington's part, or on the part of his new secretary of state, Edmund Randolph (who had recently replaced Jefferson), remains unclear, but in London Jay was operating well beyond the parameters narrowly described in Monroe's instructions.

The relationship between Monroe and Jay was complicated to begin with, because Monroe had helped organize opposition in the Senate to Jay's appointment to the London embassy. Both Washington and Randolph apparently concluded that these wounds would have healed sufficiently for Monroe and Jay to collaborate as required, or perhaps they did not particularly see the necessity of the two men getting along with each other.

Having established the aim of close relations with France, Monroe's instructions became more explicit. He was to address the claims of American citizens arising from French seizure of American ships, and he was to seek French support in acquiring navigation rights on the Mississippi River.

After some delay, Monroe was received at the French National Convention. At his accreditation ceremony, Monroe's written address, in the form of a letter to the convention, and letters from the houses of Congress were read. These "expressions of fraternity and union between the two peoples, and the interest which the United States takes in the French Republic are heard with a lively sensibility and with applause," according to the records of this ceremony, and "in witness of the fraternity which unites these two peoples, French and American, the President [of the Convention] gives the *accolade* to Citizen Monroe."[15]

Monroe's written address was, to say the least, a warm one: "Republics should approach near to each other. In many respects they all have the same interest. But this is more especially the case with the American and French Republics—their governments are similar; they both cherish the same principles and rest on the same basis, the equal and unalienable rights of man."[16] Washington expressed disapproval of Monroe's fervent, but measured, address to the convention as not being "well devised." Jay found it "disagreeable" to the British, and Randolph, in what amounted to an official censure, chastised Monroe for the "extreme glow" of some parts of his introductory remarks. Monroe had abruptly received his introduction to the treacherous challenges of U.S. diplomacy.

In a letter to Madison, Monroe asserted that American politics were at work. He concluded that the Federalists were using him to have it both ways; they wanted the French to have a perception of close ties to the United States, but only privately so as not to offend the British. Clearly there was confusion in Philadelphia. Even after chastising Monroe, Secretary of State Randolph immediately sent a second letter, exhorting him to "remove every suspicion of our preferring a connexion with Great Britain, or in any manner weakening our old attachment to France." "Small wonder," concludes the historian Harry Ammon, "that Monroe continued to regard the tightening of Franco-American relations as the primary objective of his mission, whereas the president wished only to preserve the status quo."[17] For his part, Monroe wrote to Madison, he was happy to have communications of U.S.-French friendship public so that they could not later be disavowed if the British took offense. After all, his instructions had said nothing about showing "our confidence in the French Republic" secretly. Monroe's split political personality began to emerge, "attempting at one and the same time to serve as a spokesman for his government and to act as a political leader seeking victory for his party."[18] Caught in this tension, Monroe either demonstrated the genuine confusion of a diplomatic naif or used his ministry to thwart the pro-British ambitions of the Federalists. In either case, he was courting trouble.

And further trouble came quickly. In a communication to the revolutionary Committee of Public Safety, Monroe raised the issue of French interference with British products on American ships in violation of the commercial treaty of 1778. But he did so apologetically and so humbly that the French would feel under no legal obligation to comply. The French, after the passage of four months, passed their own decree of compliance with the treaty, but not before Monroe found himself again in hot water with both Washington and Randolph, who let him know of their displeasure at his leniency.

Monroe soon also found himself enmeshed in a spiderweb of Parisian rumors and international intrigue about Jay's mission to London, which had led to the Jay Treaty being signed in London on November 19, 1794, just three months after Monroe's accreditation to the French. Under the terms of the treaty Jay had negotiated, the United States agreed not to retaliate against Great Britain commercially for a decade, in exchange for which Great Britain agreed to relinquish its forts on the American side of the Great Lakes and to provide limited access of U.S. merchant ships to the West Indies trade. The treaty also agreed to arbitration of ship seizures, compensation for Loyalists' claims, payment of prewar American debt to Great Britain, and resolution of certain Canadian border disputes. The debate over the merits of this treaty inflamed disputes between Federalist and Republican congressional factions and spread to the public at large, contributing substantially to the organization of these factions into something like political parties.[19]

Exchanges between Jay, a stalwart Federalist, and Monroe in the weeks that followed seesawed back and forth over whether Monroe had a right to know the actual terms of the treaty, and if so, whether he was at liberty to share them with the French, who had immediately suspected treachery by the Americans and the British. Given Monroe's role in organizing Senate opposition to Jay's appointment to the London mission, the relationship could not have been a good one to begin with. Jay first told Monroe that nothing in the treaty affected the United States' relations with the French, then wrote that, when Monroe received the terms of the treaty, he was to keep them confidential. In the meantime, based on Jay's prior promise that nothing in the treaty "shall be construed to operate contrary to existing treaties between the United States and other powers," Monroe had unwisely promised the French that he would disclose the terms of the treaty as soon as he had obtained them.

Monroe was now keenly stretched between his duties as an emissary and diplomat, on the one hand, and his strong feelings as a political partisan on the other. "Further and further," writes one historian, "Monroe found himself entangled in the unfortunate web his strong partisanship had woven. Here was a diplomat, ostensibly at his post to maintain his country's neutrality, in its best interests, yet acting in a manner likely . . . 'to range him with the French government as the aggrieved party in opposition to Jay and, consequently, to the government of the United States.' "[20]

Throughout the spring and summer of 1795, correspondence among Jay, Monroe, Randolph, and a series of official and unofficial intermediaries continued, as did Monroe's exchange of letters with Madison, especially over the implications and deeper meanings of the Jay Treaty and how it should be interpreted in light of U.S.-French relations. This era of confusion and intrigue finally ended in August of that year when Paris newspapers obtained and printed the full text of the treaty. Monroe took the terms of the treaty apart in correspondence with Madison but was officially obliged to argue to the French that its terms in no way affected the strong ties between America and France. Finally, in February 1796, the French foreign minister berated Monroe and concluded that the treaty constituted a breach in the alliance between France and the United States.

President Washington was not without some responsibility for the heightened bitterness between the American factions and for the confusion, at best, with the two European powers. He selected an Anglophile, Jay, to negotiate with the British and a Francophile, Monroe, to negotiate with the French and then "tried to steer a course between these enthusiasms and dangers."[21] This task was not made easier by his secretary of the treasury, Hamilton, communicating secretly with the British minister to the United States and his former secretary of state, Jefferson, receiving confidential communications from Monroe in Paris and both agitating directly and through house journalists against the intentions of the other.

Monroe had used the months in the interim to press the United States' interests in navigation rights on the Mississippi, and he urged the French in their negotiation of a peace treaty with Spain to include these interests in the final agreement. Since Monroe had acted as an unofficial interlocutor for the Spanish with the French in moving the peace negotiations forward, the Spanish were inclined to accede. On October 27, 1795, the Treaty of San Lorenzo el Real included provisions granting the United States freedom of navigation on the Mississippi with limited rights to the use of the port of New Orleans. During the same period, Monroe also used his access to the councils of the French revolutionary government to distribute summaries of the U.S. Constitution and to urge France (unsuccessfully) to adopt it as a model for a new French constitution then being drafted.

If the U.S. government in Philadelphia needed any further evidence for the recall of its minister to France, in the aftermath of Monroe's failure (or, better, refusal) to convince the French that the Jay Treaty was benign, it was afforded in the form of Monroe's hospitality to the flamboyant Thomas Paine. Though an ardent revolutionary, Paine had complained to the Directory against the execution of the French king and had been incarcerated in the Luxembourg prison for his troubles. Monroe secured his release and gave him lodgings on the condition that Paine refrain from pamphleteering against U.S. policy. Paine returned Monroe's hospitality by promptly using confidential conversations with Monroe as grist for his anti-Washington mill.

Monroe's superiors had finally had enough. Three cabinet officers, with Hamilton in support, convinced Washington that Monroe's failure to sell the Jay Treaty to the French was grounds for recall. "A minister who has thus made the notorious enemies of the whole system of the [U.S.] government his confidential correspondents in matters which affect that government, cannot be relied on to do his duty to the latter," the cabinet officers wrote to the president. For his part, though he believed he had provided a great service by postponing the harsh French response to the Jay Treaty for many months, Monroe saw the recall coming but refused to resign to please the Federalists, once again imposing American political conflict on complex diplomacy.

In November 1796, Monroe's letter of recall arrived, citing President Washington's "uneasiness and dissatisfaction" with his mission and mentioning "other concurring circumstances." Preparing for his departure, Monroe expressed his sentiments to the French Assembly: "It was my fortune to arrive among you in a moment of complicated danger from within and from without; and it is with the most heartfelt satisfaction that in taking my leave, I behold victory and the dawn of prosperity upon the point of realizing the great objects for which . . . you have . . . so nobly contended."[22] In response the French president-director, Paul de Barras, concluded that France "would not abase herself by calculating the consequences of the condescension of the American government to the suggestions of her former tyrants," by which he meant the British. Addressing Monroe, Barras concluded: "As for you, Mr. minister plenipotentiary, you have combated for principles. You have known the true interests of your country. Depart with our regret. In you we give up a representative to America, and retain the remembrance of the citizen whose personal qualities did honor to that title."[23]

In retrospect, Monroe's diplomatic error lay less in his promotion of strong Franco-American ties and more in his superimposition of domestic American political struggles between Federalists and Republicans onto a complex European scene. He insisted on seeing, not totally inaccurately, the European world of the late eighteenth century in almost Manichaean terms: good republican France and bad monarchical Britain. Washington wanted to stay above it all, having favor with Britain and France. Jefferson would tack back and forth depending on the circumstances of the day, favoring one today and another tomorrow. Madison would reap the consequences of playing one off against the other. In some ways, it was left to Monroe as eventual president to sort through the diplomatic rubble in an effort to achieve secure borders for an expanding nation.

Perhaps the most revealing evidence of Monroe the man in this whole experience came while the Jay Treaty awaited ratification in the U.S. Senate. During this period Monroe conveyed to Secretary of State Randolph a rugged foreign policy view that would become his hallmark and would set him apart from his Republican mentors: "the insults and injuries of Britain are to be no longer borne, and . . . we ought to seek redress by again appealing to arms"; more specifically, he advocated opening American access to the Mississippi by force. To Madison he wrote that the United States should invade Canada and occupy the Bermudas to force its claims against Great Britain. According to Monroe's biographer Harry Ammon:

> This vigorous approach . . . became a cardinal principle in his view of American foreign policy. Again and again he was to restate these conclusions during the next two decades, only to find that such aggressive counsel was no more to the liking of his Republican associates than it had been to Washington and the Federalists. As Samuel Flagg Bemis observed, "Monroe is

unique among the early national leaders in that his writings are free from those constant affirmations that the true policy of the United States was to steer clear of European politics." From a very early date Monroe envisaged a far more active role for the United States in the world scene as the sole way of safe-guarding American interests.[24]

This view supports an interpretation of Monroe as a leader unafraid to exert power in the national interest and vigorous in his promotion of American interests. His early inclinations in this regard would carry over into his presidency, where issues of national security, territorial expansion, and border protection were foremost.

Upon Monroe's return from Paris in 1797, after spending time in New York seeking redress from the new secretary of state, Timothy Pickering, for what he felt was unjustified recall from his post in Paris, the former envoy made his way back to Virginia. He spent considerable time writing letters to friends and a pamphleteering appeal for justice to his fellow Americans that strongly suggested he, and the interests of the United States in friendship with France, had been sacrificed by the administration's ambitions for closer relations with Great Britain. His low spirits could not have been helped by counterattacks led by President John Adams, who commented, in a speech on the warm farewell given Monroe by the French government, "that the honor done, the publicity and solemnity given to the audience of leave to a disgraced minister [Monroe], recalled in displeasure for misconduct, was a studied insult to the government of my country."[25]

An angry exchange of letters with Secretary of State Pickering left Monroe even more distressed until, finally, with the advice and support of both Jefferson and Madison, he wrote a 407-page defense of his mission to France with the formidable title "A View of the Conduct of the Executive in the Foreign Affairs of the United States Connected with the Mission to the French Republic During the Years 1794, 5 & 6." In his sixty-page introduction, he indicted the Washington administration for not cultivating the friendship of France, which he considered to be very much in the interest of the United States. He argued that the U.S. government should have been wise enough to secure French aid on behalf of American claims against Great Britain, and had it done so, "it would never have been necessary to sign a humiliating peace treaty with the ancient enemy of the nation."[26] For Washington, stung sufficiently by Monroe's criticisms to make forty pages of marginal notes, the "View" represented a final breach with his former lieutenant. Jefferson judged the work "masterly."

At this relatively early stage of his political career, James Monroe began to demonstrate a pattern of behavior that would characterize his relations with many friends and colleagues and represent one of the few shortcomings in his character. Monroe took offense readily. His skin, in modern parlance, was thin. He became especially prickly when his conduct was questioned or his judgment second-guessed. It did not matter whether his critic was a famous president (Washington) or a friend who happened to be president (Jefferson) or a peer to whom he was subordinate (Madison). Monroe felt almost all criticism or disagreement to be a challenge to his intelligence, judgment, or rectitude. Once challenged, Monroe rarely sulked. He instead defended his performance, usually in writing. The inevitable result of his inability to brush aside his critics, including his superiors, was friction. Monroe was inclined to risk lifelong attachments and friendships in defense of his character. And that is what the friction almost always seemed to involve in Monroe's mind—not a question of judgment but a question of character. He wore his honor on his sleeve and was quick to believe it tarnished. It is something of a tribute to his other attributes that his relationships largely survived his excessive sensitivity. Nevertheless, during service in three presidential administrations, Monroe found himself at odds with those he had been called upon to serve whenever they questioned his performance of his duties.

Back in Virginia, Monroe had long wanted his principal residence to be nearer to that of Jefferson, and after his confrontation with Washington and Pickering he constructed a serviceable house on the acreage adjacent to Monticello. However, his hopes for a grander home, perhaps along the lines of Jefferson's magnificent creation, could not be realized owing to his difficult financial situation.

In Monroe's day, compensation for public officials was insufficient to cover all the costs of public service. Monroe, like others, had insufficient sources of private income. Thus, when he returned from Paris he was already in debt, and the debts would mount throughout his life until, "on his retirement from the Presidency he was on the verge of ruin," in the assessment of Harry Ammon.[27] Returning to the law practice helped only slightly, for Federalist lawyers had greater hopes of prosperity and Monroe was decidedly a Republican.

Restless when he practiced law or farmed for long, Monroe permitted, perhaps encouraged, his name to be submitted to the Virginia Assembly, and at age forty-one he was elected governor of the commonwealth. The news reached George Washington some days later, and, after responding angrily, he caught cold and soon died. Not too long thereafter Monroe's only son contracted one of many prevalent childhood diseases and, despite frantic efforts to save him, also died.

During 1799–1800 the Federalist party, divided between forces behind Adams and those behind Hamilton, began an ultimately fatal disintegration. As Adams's vice president, Jefferson stood removed. Madison chose not to seek advantage. Monroe, the most traditionally political of the three, began to fill the vacuum. He foresaw, perhaps as clearly as anyone on the scene, the epic battle for political power about to be fought in the context of the 1800 presidential election, one that Jefferson, the eventual victor, would call "the second American revolution."

In correspondence with Jefferson in early 1801, Monroe warned with considerable alarm and vehemence of a rumored scheme to preempt Jefferson's apparant electoral victory by appointing John Marshall, or another likely alternative, to the presidency to prevent a vote in the House of Representatives that would give the presidency to Jefferson. Monroe described this period as being "critical and alarming" and even suggested a pony express communication system between the capital and Williamsburg so the Virginians could keep abreast of rapidly evolving political manipulations. Jefferson himself, whether reflecting Monroe's alarm or influenced by separate sources of information, wrote Monroe that should any effort at usurpation occur he would advocate a declaration "openly and firmly, one and all, that the day such an act passed, the middle States would arm, & that no such usurpation, even for a single day should be submitted to." Happily, these fears proved not to have sufficient foundation to warrant action, and Jefferson was inaugurated in March 1801.

As governor, Monroe sought to bring more activism to his position than the powers of the office could bear. By design it was a weak position, but Monroe tried with little success to introduce state social initiatives and reforms to a conservative planter legislature. Nevertheless, the editor of the *Richmond Enquirer* concluded that "he erected the negative functions of a governor into the instruments of a most respectable influence." Monroe took a particularly Jeffersonian view of the centrality of public education to the proper functioning of a republic. To the legislature he wrote: "In a government founded on the sovereignty of the people the education of youth is an object of the first importance. . . . A people well informed on the subject of their rights, their interests, and their duties would never fall into the excesses which proved the ruin of the ancient republicks."[28] Likewise, in the classic republican vein, he advocated for state support for training and equipping the militia as the bulwark of homeland security and managed to persuade the legislature to finance a state-owned armory to supply the local militia with weapons.

After three years as governor, Monroe retired. Not too long thereafter, he received an urgent communication from President Jefferson asking him to undertake another diplomatic assignment: the acquisition of the Floridas and New Orleans, a transaction that became known as the Louisiana Purchase. Jefferson recognized that

Monroe's previous years in Paris, though diplomatically unsuccessful, had produced some potentially useful goodwill. And Monroe's service to Jefferson in the following five years abroad, more than any other frame of reference, offers insight into their relationship.

In May 1801, Spain had transferred the vast Louisiana Territory to Napoleonic France, presenting the new president, Jefferson, with the prospect of a more aggressive European power on the American continent, which could complicate, among other things, navigation on the Mississippi and access to the port of New Orleans. Jefferson's response was to nominate Monroe, on January 11, 1803, as envoy extraordinaire to France to seek a commercial resolution of these potential conflicts. Not surprisingly, both men saw the issue in partisan terms, suspecting the Federalists once again of seeking political advantage out of any confrontation with France. Writing decades later, Henry Adams quotes Jefferson's uncharacteristically dramatic communication to Monroe insisting on his undertaking and completing this mission.

> All eyes, all hopes, are now fixed on you; and were you to decline, the chagrin would be universal, and would shake under your feet the high ground on which you stand with the public. Indeed, I know nothing which would produce such a shock, for on the event of this mission [purchasing Louisiana] depend the future destinies of this Republic. If we cannot, by a purchase of this country, insure to ourselves a course of perpetual peace and friendship with all nations, then, as war cannot be distant, it behooves us to be preparing for that course, without hastening it, and it may be necessary, on your failure on the Continent, to cross the Channel [to Britain]. We shall get entangled in European politics, and, figuring more, be much less happy and prosperous.[29]

Shortly before Monroe's departure to Paris, Jefferson had further evidenced his confidence in words the younger man could not soon forget: "Some men are born for the public. Nature, by fitting them for the service of the human race on a broad scale, has stamped them with the evidences of destination and their duty."

Returning to Paris after seven years, Monroe had to insert himself into ongoing negotiations between the French government and the American minister Robert Livingston, negotiations into which Napoleon himself, through his minister Talleyrand, had introduced an offer to the United States of the entire Louisiana Territory, not merely the town of New Orleans for which Livingston had been bargaining. There was no consensus between Jefferson and his envoys Livingston and Monroe. "Livingston and Monroe wanted the President to seize West Florida, and negotiate for East Florida," Henry Adams writes; "Jefferson preferred to negotiate for West Florida and to leave East Florida alone for the time."[30]

Napoleon's startling offer—"I renounce Louisiana"—stunned Livingston. "Naturally," Henry Adams writes, "Livingston for a moment lost countenance." The dumbfounded Livingston's response— "I told him no"—is surely as great a lesson against the folly of strict adherence to instruction as exists in the history of international diplomacy. When Monroe was presented to Napoleon at dinner on May 1, 1803, the French leader asked him questions about Jefferson: Was he married? Did he have children? Did he live in the national capital? Napoleon accurately predicted another war between the Americans and British and observed, "Our affairs [the matter of Louisiana] should be settled." Having been instructed to acquire East and West Florida and New Orleans, Monroe now found himself bidding for all of the Louisiana Territory, including the Floridas. However, France denied ownership of the Floridas, claiming that they still belonged to Spain.

Though Monroe had successfully completed, at least in principle, the acquisition of Louisiana, the next logical step would have been for him to proceed to Spain to negotiate for the Floridas, but his instructions were to go to London to explore a possible defense alliance that would protect the commercial activities of the United States, as a neutral nation, from British impressments of American seamen. Monroe remained in London for more than a year, from July 1803 until the late fall of 1804. Yet he accomplished little. The amity that prevailed at the British court toward America was superficial, undercut by grievances, petty and great, and by lingering British contempt for its former colonies.

Having failed to make any real headway in London, Monroe was finally instructed to proceed to Spain, by way of Paris, to try to resolve the issue of acquisition of the Floridas. Back in Paris, Livingston pressed upon Monroe the unlikely argument that France had initially possessed West Florida and probably East Florida as part of its original acquisition of Louisiana, and therefore that Spain should be persuaded to relinquish any claims to the Floridas in favor of the United States as the new owners of Louisiana. The argument required France's concurrence to a claim of ownership it had not heretofore ever made. According to the inimitable Henry Adams, this argument would have further required U.S. negotiators to claim "that Spain had retroceded West Florida to France without knowing it, and that France, in ignorance of its involuntary ownership, had transferred her rights to the United States, that the United States had bought it without paying for it, and that neither France nor Spain . . . were competent to decide the meaning of their own contract."[31]

Arriving in Madrid on this complicated mission on January 2, 1805, Monroe encountered a diplomatic briar patch rivaled only by the ones he had just left in London and Paris. The U.S. minister, Charles Pinckney, a converted Federalist, had undertaken extraordinary measures, including clumsy threats of force, to alienate the Spanish government. The long list of issues brought by Monroe to be resolved between Spain and the United States, not least territorial disputes around New Orleans, in West Florida, and along the Rio Bravo, required the support of the United States' position by France. The Spanish, having learned that the French had no intention of providing such support, treated Monroe haughtily, and after almost six months in Madrid he withdrew yet again in frustration and defeat.

Returning to London, he spent the next year and a half seeking to negotiate resolution of a variety of bilateral issues, most of which related to the seemingly irresolvable matter of impressments and of rights of commerce and trade. These matters were cast against a backdrop of international power politics—largely focused on the Franco-British struggle—around which the perceived interests of the United States vacillated during the second Jefferson administration. Monroe was confronted with the sight of American prize ships being towed into British ports. Jefferson shifted his focus from obtaining a U.S.-British alliance to establishing rapprochement with France with the goal, possibly with the assistance of some ready cash, of obtaining the elusive Floridas. Little diplomatic or political daylight appeared between Jefferson and Monroe throughout this period. Unlike the earlier mission to France, where Washington believed Monroe to be playing fast and loose with his instructions, in this case Monroe clearly exceeded the letter of his instructions, and exhibited characteristic (even spectacular) independence, principally in the acquisition of Louisiana from Napoleon. But the consequences were so extraordinarily favorable to the United States, and received with equally extraordinary acclaim from its citizens, that Jefferson, who received the credit, was not inclined to complain.

Early in 1806, however, politics did rear an ugly countenance in the form of a schism among the Republicans, fostered in this case by John Randolph of Roanoke, a Jefferson enemy. Alleging that Jefferson and Madison now designed foreign policy, with regard to both Great Britain and France, in such a way as to guarantee Madison's succession to the presidency, Randolph privately and publicly called on Monroe to return and challenge Madison for the presidency. Responding to Randolph, Monroe turned aside the overture (at least for the time being) in favor of maintaining his long-standing ties to both Jefferson and Madison. Jefferson had warned him, "Some of your new friends [Randolph and company] are attacking your old ones [himself and Madison] out of friendship for you, but in a way to render you great injury."[32] Noting Jefferson's unhappiness with Randolph's intriguing, Henry Adams wrote that Jefferson "had never found fault with intrigue so long as he had a share in it. . . . the President, who was a master of intrigue, used the weapon freely to defend his favorite [Madison] and himself."

In the midst of this domestic political intrigue, in collaboration with the envoy William Pinckney, Monroe successfully negotiated a treaty meant to resolve a variety of commercial conflicts between Great Britain and the United States, but it was rejected by Jefferson for its failure to include guarantees against British impressments of U.S. seamen. Here Jefferson and his envoy strongly disagreed. Jefferson wanted formal commitments by the British against impressments in the body of the treaty; Monroe contended that the British would refuse on principle to abandon impressments but would yield in practice. Even though Jefferson rejected this hard-won treaty, he was now tilting toward England in its contest with France. He wrote to Monroe that "an English ascendancy on the ocean is safer for us than that of France." Caught up in global power politics, the lesser power, in this case the United States, could afford to set ideological affinities aside in favor of national interest. Besides which, Napoleonic France was not the revolutionary republic so dear to American Republicans.

From a variety of sources, not least the Federalist press, Monroe was informed that Jefferson had rejected his diplomatic efforts as a means of cultivating anti-British public opinion behind his secretary of state, James Madison, as his successor. Because John Randolph was trying to draft Monroe to oppose Madison, and was using these sources to persuade Monroe to stand against Madison for president, Monroe had reason to believe his best efforts were being used against him. Instead of explaining his opposition to the treaty on the basis of its substance, Jefferson, citing "the wicked efforts" of the Federalist papers, chose to write to Monroe to deny these political motives: "I have before assured you that a sense of duty, as well as of delicacy would prevent me from ever expressing a sentiment on the subject [elevating Madison over Monroe]; and that I think you know me well enough to be assured I shall conscientiously observe the line of conduct I profess."

According to Henry Adams, "The blow to Monroe's pride was great, and shook his faith in the friendship with Jefferson and Madison. Three years had elapsed since he had himself been sent abroad to share Livingston's negotiations, and he had the best reason to know how easily the last comer could carry away the prizes of popularity."[33]

Finally, after almost five years abroad in his second series of diplomatic missions, Monroe returned to the United States, to the last year of the Jefferson presidency and the election of James Madison, and to the evolution of a relationship with Madison made more complex by disagreement over the failed treaty of 1806 and their competing ambitions. This entire period was not a pleasant one for James Monroe. "Since signing the Louisiana treaty, in May, 1803, he had met only with defeat and disaster," Henry Adams observed. "Insulted by every successive Foreign Secretary in France, Spain, and England; driven from Madrid to Paris and from Paris to London; set impossible tasks; often contrary to his own judgment,—he had ended by yielding to the policy of the British government, and by meeting with disapproval and disavowal from his own. . . . In many respects, Monroe's career was unparalleled, but he was singular above all in the experience of being disowned by two Presidents as strongly opposed to each other as Washington and Jefferson, and of being sacrificed by two secretaries as widely different as Timothy Pickering and James Madison."[34]

The refusal of President Jefferson and Secretary of State Madison to accept his efforts to negotiate a treaty with Great Britain that would resolve maritime and trade-related issues between the two nations—and possibly avoid the war that would follow—on the grounds that they did not also achieve guarantees from the British against impressments exercised against American ships had caused Monroe great distress. Though he was treated much more warmly than he had been by the Washington administration, and

no allegations were even suggested of malfeasance or misperfor-
mance, his failure to satisfy his two closest political allies or to persuade them to ratify his efforts became the source of personal
chagrin and disappointment.

This experience also revealed much about James Monroe the
man. According to his biographer Harry Ammon, Monroe's "most
conspicuous failing was an excessive *amour-propre*, which did not
emerge as vanity, but rather in the form of undue sensitivity to criticism. Operating as he did with such an elevated sense of his own
integrity, he could not easily adjust when old friends failed to
approve his conduct." In the case of the rejection of the treaty with
Great Britain, the source of his friction with Jefferson and Madison:
"His extreme self-consciousness about the purity of the motives
upon which his actions had been based led him to regard the rejection . . . as a direct reflection upon his character and ability."[35]

Madison's own ambitions, and whatever role Jefferson played in
fostering them, contributed to a realignment of the relationships
among Jefferson and Madison and Monroe. This realignment did
not represent a rupture or breach but did, at least for a time, create
a degree of coolness and distance. It also, to a significant extent, further identified Monroe as his own man. He was sufficiently his own
man by the fall of 1808 to permit his name to be placed in contention with that of Madison for the presidency in a contest that
represented as much a schism between new and old Republicans as
a division in the country. Madison, of course, prevailed, and it
would take the better part of two years, much behind-the-scenes
politicking, continuous interventions here and there by Jefferson,
and some diplomacy on Monroe's part to bring him back into his
party's good graces.

After standing, unsuccessfully, against Madison for the presidency, Monroe turned his attention in the fall of 1809 to his 2,800-
acre estate at Albemarle near Monticello and his other property in
Loudoun County, Virginia. His plans to sell at least a portion of the
Loudoun County property to finance improvements at Albemarle
were defeated by depressed land prices, so he borrowed ten

thousand dollars, a considerable sum in those days, for improvements on the Albemarle plantation.[36] His earlier plans to rent a
house in Richmond and practice law there were soon abandoned in
favor of rural life. At Albemarle the Monroes inhabited a plain
house they called the Highlands. For some historians, this move farther into Virginia's interior represented a clear symbolic break by
Monroe, following Jefferson, with the East of plantations and European manners in favor of the woodsmen and pioneers at the
foothills of the Allegheny mountain range. Like his neighbor Jefferson, Monroe experimented with novel horticultural techniques,
some gained in Europe, to help improve crop yields of grain as a
replacement for tobacco, whose value was steadily declining.

In September 1808 the Monroes' older daughter, Eliza, had married Judge George Hay, twenty years her senior and a prominent
lawyer and political figure. Hay would become his father-in-law's
close political adviser through the presidency, and he and Eliza
would live with the Monroes in the White House during large portions of the Monroe administration. Maria Hester, the much younger
Monroe daughter, was only six when the first Monroe grandchild,
Hortensia Hay, was born a year after Eliza's wedding. Monroe presented the Hays a small estate called Ashfield near Richmond.

During 1809–10 Monroe performed a balancing act: he had one
foot inside the political arena trying to reestablish his party standing and one foot in the private sector trying to restore his finances,
which once again had been eroded by lengthy diplomatic service
abroad. Monroe and Madison saw little of each other during this
early period of the Madison administration, with the exception of a
reconciliation in Washington in May 1810, described by one
observer as "kind and friendly."

Monroe reestablished his party's confidence by being elected to
the Virginia House of Delegates in April 1810, and he was then
successfully put forward for governor of Virginia and elected on
January 16, 1811. His tenure was brief, for on March 14, Madison
inquired, through an intermediary, whether Monroe would consider serving as his secretary of state. The key issue still standing

between them was the split between Monroe and the Jefferson administration over the aborted 1806 treaty with Great Britain. An intricate, nuanced exchange of correspondence, almost impenetrable in the delicacy of its language, permitted a face-saving reconciliation, described by Monroe's biographer Harry Ammon as follows:

To Monroe's inquiry whether the President was willing to work with a person whose policy views had recently differed from those of the administration, Madison gave his assurance that this did not constitute an obstacle; the situation was still fluid and a change might be possible if circumstances altered. Monroe had not demanded a pledge about the future course of the administration. He had received what he had most wanted, an acknowledgment of the rectitude of his conduct in 1806.[37]

This new rapprochement led to Monroe's eventual occupation of the two most important cabinet positions simultaneously in the second Madison administration, and to his own eventual succession to the presidency. Though abroad during much of the Jefferson presidency, Monroe maintained close contact with Jefferson, as friend, political ally, and emissary, to the degree the glacial transatlantic communications systems of the day permitted. With Madison, the early cordial relationship turned more complex and more professional, for both Madison as president and Monroe as secretary of state were constantly absorbed in issues between the United States and Britain, and to a degree with France and other powers, largely relating to trade, duties and tariffs, maritime conflicts, access to ports, illegal blockades, harassment of shipping, impressments, and a tangle of intricate commercial, diplomatic, and ultimately military frictions.

All evidence suggests close cooperation between the president and his secretary of state, concurring that British intransigence on a whole range of outstanding American complaints, repeatedly

sidestepped by British emissaries and their government, were leading the two nations closer to war. Since little written correspondence between Madison and Monroe was required during this
period, documentation of their relationship is all secondhand and
reveals few serious policy differences. Indeed, Monroe himself gave
the best description of this relationship to one correspondent: "The
conduct of P. [Madison] since my arrival has corresponded with our
antient [sic] relation, which I am happy to have restor'd. On publick affairs we confer without reserve, each party expressing his
own sentiments, and viewing dispassionately the existing state, ani-
mated by a sincere desire to promote the public welfare. I have full
confidence that this relation will be always preserved in future."[38]

Under pressure from war hawks in the House of Representatives, in his annual message to Congress in November 1811, President Madison proposed "putting the United States into an armor
and an attitude demanded by the crisis," and asked Congress to raise
an auxiliary military force and increase the size of the navy. Monroe
was given the duty of guiding Madison's initiatives through Congress and he "proved his worth by providing the President with an
effective liaison with congressional leaders."[39]

Monroe's entry into the Madison cabinet, according to one historian, "made a resolution of the long Anglo-American controversy
inevitable; if a settlement could not be arranged [of long-standing
disputes over commercial and maritime rights], then the nation
must protect its rights with force."[40] In the months that followed,
the new secretary of state was extensively involved in negotiations
with the ministers of France and Great Britain in trying to resolve
these intricate, time-consuming maritime and commercial disputes,
but to little avail. The United States had grievances against both
nations, grievances that resisted resolution. It did not help that each
of these European powers sought to manipulate its negotiations
with the United States to gain advantage against the other.

In his treatment of James Madison's presidency, Garry Wills
assesses Monroe's original role in the cabinet: "Monroe, before
accepting Madison's offer to become secretary of state, had

demanded that he would be a full partner in the administration, not simply a mouthpiece for Madison's views. This could have meant that Monroe would lead Madison back toward friendly relations with England—Monroe had, after all, struck a treaty with England that would have allowed impressments. But Monroe in fact brought a more warlike attitude into the cabinet."[41] In fact, the treaty Monroe negotiated was premised on Great Britain abandoning impressments in practice, but warlike Monroe certainly turned out to be. In responding to Madison's offer of the Department of State, Monroe wrote: "I was sincerely of opinion, after the failure of negotiation with Spain, or rather France, that it was for the interest of our country, to make an accommodation with England, the great maritime power, even on moderate terms, rather than hazard war, or any other alternative. . . . I own that I have since seen no cause to doubt its soundness."[42]

Hand in hand, Madison and Monroe marched the nation to war against England, largely on the seemingly insoluble issue of British impressments of American seamen. In June 1812, both houses of Congress approved Madison's resolution of war; some congressmen, based on mounting anti-French sentiment in the United States, argued that war with France also be declared. This, wisely, was resisted.

By now Monroe had seven years of his life invested in attempted resolution of Anglo-American disputes. Once war became the only recourse, Monroe's martial instincts took over. He wanted to abandon the useless tools of diplomacy and take up the sword. "Monroe chafed at continuing in the State Department, now a post of secondary importance," Ammon notes. "A military command seemed a much more satisfactory way of serving the nation."[43]

Madison, however, resisted the notion of giving Monroe a command senior to other serving officers. And Monroe's romantic notion of raising a Virginia regiment under his command was abandoned, on advice of friends, because "many would conclude that he had such an insatiable thirst for military glory that he was willing to sacrifice the interests of the nation." Instead, in 1814 the ineffective secretary of war, William Eustis, was persuaded to resign, and Monroe became acting secretary of war, leaving the State Department duties to Richard Rush. Meanwhile, as secretary of state Monroe readily welcomed an offer from Czar Alexander I of Russia, conveyed through his future secretary of state and current U.S. minister to Russia, John Quincy Adams, to mediate the Anglo-American dispute.

"All looked to Monroe, who was considered the only member of the Cabinet with any knowledge of military affairs, as the ideal replacement" for Eustis, according to Ammon.[44] His appointment to head the War Department as its official secretary was not resisted by Monroe, as Garry Wills suggests, because it might turn into a hash and impede his chances for the presidency. Instead, his appointment met Senate resistance based not on his competence but, as Wills concurs, on the fact he was a Virginian in an age when Virginians seemed overwhelmingly dominant on the national scene. Monroe was therefore named acting secretary as a compromise. After a few weeks, he was replaced by a permanent secretary of war, John Armstrong, a bitter rival and continuing antagonist of Monroe's. Upon resuming his post at the State Department, Monroe could not keep away from the fray and shortly proposed a much-needed intelligence service that could track British movements and deployments, a proposal successfully resisted by Armstrong to the nation's detriment.

With the collapse of Napoleon in Europe in the spring and summer of 1814, the British found themselves free to focus their military energies on their former colonies. In an effort to forestall a British invasion of the United States, now made more likely by Napoleon's defeat, Madison appointed a commission to negotiate a peace with Britain, with the commissioners authorized to abandon the effort to seek an end to maritime impressments. Impressment had always been the sticking point, and cause for Jefferson's and Madison's rejection of the treaty Monroe had negotiated eight years before. "If Monroe felt any satisfaction in seeing the administration back at the point which had been reached in 1806, he

refrained from comment," remarks one biographer. British commanders had deployed five thousand regular troops and fifty ships
at the mouth of the Potomac with the objective of capturing the
U.S. capital. Having little intelligence, the former military officer
Monroe took a cavalry troop to reconnoiter the British, surely a first
and last for a secretary of state. But, as one historian notes, "Monroe . . . had a lifelong weakness . . . an ambition to see himself in a
leading military role."[45] Monroe's subsequent warning, sent to
Madison on August 21, that a major British force was on the move
toward Washington, enabled the president and his wife to undertake evacuation of personnel and valuable national property. When
a deputation of citizens appeared seeking Madison's approval to
surrender the capital, Madison refused and Monroe warned that if
"any deputation moved towards the enemy [for surrender] it would
be repelled by the bayonet."

The burning of the capital finally led Madison to request Armstrong's removal as secretary of war for his incompetence and his rising unpopularity. Monroe was thus made permanent secretary of war
and acting secretary of state. "Now, as Secretary of both War and
State, Monroe was given the greatest opportunity of his long career,
in the critical period following the fall of Washington, to prove his
ability," writes W. P. Cresson.[46] He promptly broke ranks with
Republican doctrine, heavily reliant on the state militias for homeland defense, and proposed conscription of a one-hundred-thousand-
man army in response to threatened British invasions from Canada
and against New Orleans. And in August 1814 Monroe successfully
organized the defeat of a superior British force at Baltimore. Thereafter Monroe relinquished his cabinet position in the War Department and resumed his responsibilities as secretary of state. But "in the
long hours he was spending with Madison attempting to restore the
prestige of the country and the administration, Monroe could not but
be keenly aware that he was mending the warp and woof of his own
battered past and gathering up the threads that would fashion the
design of his own future," according to Cresson.[47]

The exigencies of war required Madison, Monroe, and the

Republicans to question two orthodox beliefs of their political faith: conscription and a national bank. A conscription plan was drawn up, but never used, to defend the nation. And the Madison administration proposed a national bank to finance the war. Jefferson was "scandalized" by Republicans adopting a Hamiltonian plan for a national bank even more than by the nation acquiring a standing army, rather than the militia, to defend itself. But Monroe, out of a sense of desperation over the nation's financial plight, offered no resistance to the bank. "Monroe had indeed traveled a long way since the 1790s," according to his biographer Ammon. "He was the first national figure in the Republican party to understand how drastically the character of the party had altered since 1800 and to realize that it was no longer primarily agrarian in its composition. Concessions must be made to the mercantile element, which was forming an increasingly important segment of Republicanism in the Northern and Middle states."[48] Changing times and new realities required reexamination of long-held principles.

With the signing of the Treaty of Ghent in late 1814, sealed by Andrew Jackson's victory over the British at New Orleans on January 8, 1815, Monroe was free to step down as secretary of war, which he did on March 15, and resume responsibility for foreign affairs. He had been in one or both senior cabinet offices for four intensive years. It would take almost six months before he recovered his severely impaired health. Another source of personal stress for Monroe during his years as secretary of state, then secretary of war, under Madison was that he saw little of Eliza, with whom he was very close. By 1815 this separation had driven her into some sort of depression. George Hay wrote to his father-in-law, "[Eliza] actually moans over your absence. Ten times a day she repeats, if I could but see my father and dear mother *here*." Shortly thereafter, Monroe had Eliza relocated south to Albemarle in the hope that the cooler climate of the highlands might improve her condition.

Monroe's return to the capital in October 1815 brought him renewed political attention. As with Jefferson and Madison before him, the position of secretary of state was widely assumed to be a springboard to the presidency. Due to his remarkable dual service during the War of 1812, Monroe now stood in direct line of succession to Madison, with whom he continued to be on the very favorable terms that had characterized most of their long association. According to one biographer, "While Monroe never enjoyed Jefferson's great popularity in the nation, he was, nonetheless, a widely respected figure. If most of his contemporaries did not judge him to have talents comparable to those of the first two Republican Presidents, all acknowledged that his sound judgment, his administrative abilities and his long service to the nation for four decades gave him a just claim to the succession." As he prepared for his candidacy in 1816, "following the example set by Jefferson, Madison was outwardly neutral, but it was accepted that Monroe had his support."[49]

Monroe's backers began the cultivation and organization of support among members of Congress, whose caucus nomination was tantamount to election in the absence of a serious opposition party nominee. His chief competition came from the secretary of the treasury, William H. Crawford, a former U.S. senator from Georgia, who had strong support among a number of members of Congress. After weeks and months of behind-the-scenes maneuvering, the Republican caucus voted 65 to 54 to nominate Monroe over Crawford. The Federalists nominated Rufus King, a former minister to England. Monroe was elected president in 1816 by an electoral margin of 183 to 34 and was inaugurated on March 4, 1817, as the fifth president of the United States.

With the notable exception of the successful negotiation of the Louisiana Purchase, James Monroe's diplomatic career, including two extended missions abroad and service as secretary of state, was not calculated to mark him for greatness. But he would have occasion as president to resolve the pesky matter of the acquisition of Florida, with the muscular aid of General Andrew Jackson, on more favorable terms than his earlier negotiations with France and Spain yielded. Regardless of his success or failure as a diplomat, there can be little doubt that James Monroe's more than seven years' experience in Paris, London, and Madrid, and his years as secretary of state during the War of 1812, and the deep immersion in European political intrigue all those years offered, helped equip him for his later duties as president. Even more important, during these years he was the only one fortunate enough to receive tutorials under Washington, Jefferson, and Madison in international relations, character building, and American politics.

3

"We Cannot Go Back":
The Search for National Security

The era of James Monroe's presidency, from 1817 until 1825, represents, more than is ordinarily recognized, a phenomenal period. The old order dominated by great figures of the American Revolution was passing. The United States was seeking more stable definition of its relationships with the European powers. Normalization of trade and maritime relations between the United States and Europe was a continuing struggle. With the exception of the British in Canada, the claims of Great Britain, France, and Spain in North America were being reduced by negotiation and conflict. The dramatic clash of "factions," political parties represented by the Federalists and the Republicans, reached its peak in the election of 1800, "the second American revolution," and was seriously waning as schisms diminished the Federalists' ranks. The introduction of new states into the Union, especially Missouri, would raise the ugly issue of slavery and its reach. Individual settlers, then whole communities, were moving westward. In short, the United States was in transition from adolescence to young adulthood.

This transition, however, required a much greater degree of national security than the United States had enjoyed in the past. Monroe assumed the presidency in the aftermath of the War of 1812, and the British burning of the nation's capital very much seared the public imagination. Abandoned British posts in the

Northwest Territory were being garrisoned by American forces. There was turbulence in the Southeast due to Seminole unrest, pirate activities, and the absence of a strong Spanish administration. Rights of navigation on western rivers were still in some dispute. Settlers demanded protection not only from Indians resisting their encroachment but also from foreign claims of sovereignty. The claims of the United States and Russia to areas of the coastal Northwest were in dispute. Finally, there was the broader hemispheric issue of revolutions in the Spanish colonies of South America and the question of U.S. support for fledgling republics to the south.

Security for the United States required resolution of all these matters. And, more than anything else, their resolution would both occupy and characterize the Monroe administration. Before he was a politician or a diplomat, James Monroe was a soldier. As he assumed ever higher public offices, his early military experience naturally affected his outlook and judgments about future security issues. As early as the spring of 1784, when he was a member of the Confederation Congress, Monroe took an active role on the issue of garrisoning British posts in the Northwest yielded by the treaty of peace following the Revolutionary War. In the words of his biographer Harry Ammon:

> His solution—the creation of a permanent military force under the control of the Congress—was highly unpalatable to many delegates, who saw the specter of tyranny in the formation of a standing army in peacetime. Monroe was not unsympathetic with this apprehension, but he considered a standing army indispensable as long as any European power held possessions on the North American continent.[1]

State militias might be adequate to deal with attacks by Indians, but "the problem presented by the presence of European powers was beyond the scope of any one state."[2]

Thus, for Monroe, security in the early United States raised a conflict between his soldierly appreciation for credible military protection and his classic republican beliefs in the dangers of a standing army. At this early stage, as well as later, he may also have reflected on his personal memories of Valley Forge and the checkered relationships between irregular militia and more reliable, better trained regular soldiers. In 1784, as well as later in life as secretary of war and president, Monroe would break with his Republican colleagues in favoring national forces for national security.

It was Jefferson who drew Monroe's attention to the West. Early in his presidency, Jefferson had written Monroe, who was then the governor of Virginia, about his vision of an America expanding to the West. Yeomen farmers would "cover the whole northern, if not southern continent, with a people speaking the same language, governed in similar forms, and by similar laws; nor can we contemplate with satisfaction either blot or mixture on that surface."[3] Jefferson and Monroe had planned a western tour back in 1784, but Jefferson's appointment by the Confederation Congress as minister to France meant that Monroe had to go alone.[4] Monroe had some land speculations in the West (as did Washington, among others), and he readily accepted Jefferson's belief that public policy toward expansion and relations with Indians required firsthand experience.

As a member of the Confederation Congress for three years, Monroe had focused on western concerns. When Congress was in recess, Monroe made two extensive western tours and, by his energy, earned a reputation as an ally of that developing region.[5] He had a personal interest, in that he had received, for his military service, a patent for five thousand acres in Kentucky and had expanded his claims well beyond that. But he also recognized the area as vital to American expansion. In the early years of the confederation, much thought was given to the various political structures that might be used to annex new organized territories. One proposal, supported by Washington (with his own personal Potomac-Ohio development) and Madison, was to annex these territories to one or another of the existing states. Another was for the territories to organize themselves into "new states," the plan favored by Jefferson and Monroe in the early 1780s. In 1783 Monroe wrote that there should be "a separation & erect an independ't State westw'd as it will enable us to oeconomize our aff'rs here & give us greater strength in the federal councils."[6] By this he meant that Virginia would not have to take on the financial burden of looking after new territory but would get the advantage of adding new southern states in the federal balance. When Jefferson left for France, Monroe took his place as the champion of the "Men of the Western Waters."[7] One biographer would conclude that "no statesman of his time played a more significant part [in western expansion] than James Monroe" and that, in his efforts to expand American claims westward, "he performed a service for which credit has too often been denied him."[8] In this capacity Monroe very much sided with the rights of the pioneers, the "men of the forest," over the interests of the eastern financiers and plantation conservatives.

Later in life, he would carry out the first presidential visit to the West, giving "westerners a new sense of confidence as they built communities beyond the mountains."[9] His interests in the West were fortified by policies designed to promote western development. In his cabinet, Secretary of War John C. Calhoun had the western portfolio, in that his department had responsibility for both frontier defense and Indian affairs. Specifically, Calhoun created an expedition to establish a military post at the mouth of the Yellowstone River on the upper Missouri River. All of Calhoun's activities were carried out with guidance from the president. Monroe also devoted considerable energy to rescuing the Indians from the relentless onslaught of westward expansion. He urged Congress to enact a plan to divide the expanse between the territories and the Rocky Mountains into districts for individual tribal resettlement, each with a civil government and school systems. In a message to Congress on March 30, 1824, Monroe proposed removal of Indian tribes within existing states to lands beyond the western boundaries, as much as anything to preserve their traditional forms of government and to permit them eventually, if they so chose, to adapt to the new America's form of government: "Land equally

good, and perhaps more fertile, may be procured for them in those
quarters. The relations between the United States and such Indians
would still be the same." He emphasized that "considerations of
humanity and benevolence" prevail.[10] Perhaps more than any other
national leader, Monroe foresaw the demand for westward expansion, first by pioneers and then, during his presidency, by a rising
tide of immigrants seeking escape from economic misery and continuing wars in Europe.

But earlier in life, as a U.S. senator in the 1790s, Monroe took
part in an effort, based on ideological fears, to block attempts by the
Washington administration to expand the regular army for protection of western interests. "This reversal of his former stand," notes
Harry Ammon, "was not the result of any change in his views on the
proper organization of frontier defense," where he had favored a
regular army presence, "but sprang from a reluctance to entrust a
larger military force to a government," including leading Federalists
such as Alexander Hamilton, whom "he distrusted."[11] It was one
thing for sound Republicans to control a standing military and
quite another for untrustworthy, ambitious Federalists to do so. He
would, within his political lifetime, reverse this position.

Some years later, in 1801, while governor of Virginia, Monroe
returned to the issue of national security from the state perspective.
In a message to the Virginia General Assembly, "Monroe touched
upon a subject in which he had long taken a particular interest—
that of national defense," according to Ammon, and emphasized
equipping the militia and providing better officer training.[12] Because
of a relatively weak national government, an ideology, and sparse
budgets, the security of the nation was still largely dependent on
state militias. Even though Virginia strongly adhered to Republican
doctrine concerning the dangers of a standing army and the need to
rely on citizen-soldiers, it was loath to increase taxes and raise revenues required to train and equip its militia. Monroe "now urged
that officers be given special training at state expense, and that the
militia regulations be thoroughly revised to shape an effective fighting force." It was one thing for Virginia gentlemen to espouse the

cause of the citizen-soldiers; it was quite another to pay the costs of proper training and equipment. Monroe's proposal, like other creative ideas he put forward, "was received with little enthusiasm, since it required a notoriously parsimonious legislature to spend money."[13]

About this time in his career, if not even earlier, James Monroe began to break with classical republican tradition, as articulated by Jefferson and others, in one historically significant way. Classic republicanism had held, since the earliest days of the Greek city-states, that a standing army in peacetime was a danger to the republic. Well into the life of the Roman Republic, the orthodox view was that maintenance of a professional military was an instrument in waiting for a monarch or oligarch (the proverbial "man on a white horse") and, further, that it eroded civic virtue by removing the duty of the citizen-soldier, the farmer-warrior, to defend the polis. Both beliefs were equally important.

America's Founders, as students of the classics, were well aware that Rome had abandoned its republican heritage and become an empire during the period when it was replacing citizen-soldiers by a professional army first and then a mercenary army sometime thereafter. The closest Monroe, a committed Republican, came to imperial ambitions was to prevent further European colonization of the Western Hemisphere. But the War of 1812 made a profound impression upon him and further convinced him that the expanding United States could no longer rely principally on state militias for its defenses. When he stepped down as secretary of war in 1815, he submitted a report to the Senate urging a larger standing army. He raised the issue of improvements to coastal fortifications, a concern he would carry with him into the White House two years later. In his report Monroe stated: "By the war we have acquired a character and rank among other nations which we did not enjoy before. We stand pledged to support this rank and character by the adoption of such measures as may evince on the part of the United States a firm resolution to do it. We cannot go back. The spirit of the nation forbids it."[14]

In other words, an expanding role for the United States in the world required it to depart from the purity of its republican heritage and face the need for dependable defenses. Scale became the crucial issue. Republics throughout history had been small—from Athens to Venice, basically city-states. The Founders had confronted the issue of scale in seeking to apply republican theory to a collective polity. They had found in the writings of Montesquieu the idea that made this possible, the idea of a federation of republics, or, to put it the other way around, a republican federation. The original states were the republics; the United States was their federated nation-state. It was an invention without precedent in history, and it enabled the Founders to preserve their republican dream. Had the United States retained its original structure, this theory might have been sustainable. But the United States was growing, and its ideal of federated republics was being challenged by a dangerous world. The expanding federal republic simply could no longer be defended by a small standing army holding off the invader until the various militias could be mustered. The fact that James Monroe was the first to confront this paradox and attempt to surmount it by itself makes him an historic figure.

Thus, as he entered the White House, Monroe was claiming a new ground beyond classic republicanism. His brand of republicanism recognized national security as a priority. As president, he would continue to pursue this idea with appeals for increased inland and coastal fortifications and expanded military forces to protect and defend the expanding perimeters of the American republic. He was ahead of his time and has received little credit for his foresight. But it required a break with the political orthodoxy in which he was schooled and with the position taken by his mentor (Jefferson) and his predecessor (Madison).

As early as the hothouse period during the prolonged election of 1800, extending into 1801, issues of domestic military force were not academic. During the razor-thin balloting in the House of Representatives between Jefferson and Burr, both sides believed the future of the Republic to be at stake, principally by resort to force by the other side. Federalists accused Republicans of preparing for armed insurrection if Burr were declared the victor. "Yet the expectation that force might be used to control the election was not restricted to Federalists; Republicans suspected that federal troops might be employed against them," writes Harry Ammon.[15] Governor Monroe received a message in February 1801 from Congressman John Tyler, who reported that twenty-two thousand men in Pennsylvania were prepared to take up arms if the Federalists claimed victory, and who urged Monroe to take steps "so that Virginia could join hands . . . to prevent a Federalist coup." Monroe took no steps to arm his state but wrote that "if anything requires decision on our part, be assured it will not be wanting."[16] As governor, Monroe was prepared to take whatever measures might be required to ensure that Jefferson's election not be stolen from him.

Years later, when James Monroe became secretary of war in the Madison administration during the War of 1812, his first act was to respond to requests from the congressional military affairs committees for a report on manpower requirements. "With an energy impressive to the most hardened congressmen," Ammon reports, "Monroe drew up a comprehensive statement of the forces needed for coastal defense and for the offensive operations planned for the summer of 1813."[17] In a detailed message to Senator George W. Campbell, chairman of the Senate Military Committee, Monroe laid out elaborate plans for defense of both coastal and inland territories, from deploying 600 troops at "Boston, including a suitable proportion of Artillery, and at Eastport, and at other posts eastward" down to deploying 100 troops in "North Carolina, one company of Artillery."[18] Earlier legislation, authorizing an additional 50,000 volunteers to augment the existing force of 35,000 men, had been ineffective because most recruits preferred service as citizen-soldiers in the state militias to full-time service for one to three years in the regular army. Congress replaced this ineffectual legislation with Monroe's plan to recruit 20,000 additional regulars on a one-year basis. Monroe proposed to use 17,000 troops to garrison important coastal cities and 4,500, to be divided between

Mobile and Savannah, to prevent the British from seizing Florida. He also proposed a 20,000-man army, with 10,000 more in reserve, for an invasion of Canada, over which he would take command with a lieutenant general's commission.

As planning for the Canadian invasion accelerated, Madison appointed as secretary of war John Armstrong, a former senator noted (by Jefferson, among others) for his intrigue, and at the time defender of New York City with the rank of brigadier. Armstrong not only suggested a lesser commission for Monroe but also declared that he intended to direct the Canadian invasion himself. Monroe's bitter complaint to Madison that the secretary of war could not also be an army commander was to no avail. In the summer of 1813 the U.S. Army took Fort George at Niagara as a prelude to a wider attack on Montreal and Quebec, but the northern invasion thereafter collapsed.

By now Armstrong and Monroe were involved in what one source called a "deadly feud." That same summer, a sizable British fleet appeared in the mouth of Chesapeake Bay. "Regarding this force as a prelude to an invasion directed against Washington," according to one historian, "Monroe urged that immediate steps be taken to strengthen the defenses of the Capital."[19] Armstrong dismissed Monroe's concerns, leaving it to the state militia in the region to defend the unfortified national capital. Monroe also urged Madison to create an intelligence capability based upon a chain of pony expresses from the Chesapeake to Washington, but this proposal was rejected by Armstrong as unnecessary. Though secretary of state, Monroe increasingly inserted himself in prewar planning and preparation and created friction with Armstrong by doing so. In December 1813 Monroe, not above intrigue against a rival, wrote President Madison that Secretary Armstrong was discussing a plan for conscription with members of Congress, seducing young officers with promises of promotion, and was agitating for measures detrimental to Madison—"an attack on the Secretary on these grounds would be an attack on you"—and continued: "if this man [Armstrong] is continued in office [he] will ruin not you and the administration only, but the whole Republican party & cause. He has already gone far to do it and it is my opinion, if he is not promptly removed, he will soon accomplish it." Monroe continued, "My advice to you is to remove him at once."[20]

Instinctively fearing British intentions, Monroe organized a small cohort of horsemen to accompany him down the Potomac River toward Chesapeake Bay. The British withdrew for the time being, and Madison had hopes, late in 1813, that peace might be mediated with the British foreign secretary, Lord Castlereagh. Even though, by the spring of 1814, Madison had revised his instructions to his negotiators, authorizing them to drop demands against impressments (the issue that had defeated Monroe's treaty with the British several years before), a peace treaty was not forthcoming. Rumors of British ship and troop concentrations in the West Indies and in Great Britain, presumably as a prelude to invasion, were dismissed by Armstrong, who refused even to order state militias to be called out and trained. When a squadron of fifty British ships, and an invasion force of five thousand regular troops, appeared at the mouth of the Potomac on August 16, Madison had finally had enough and, with Monroe, undertook the organization of the defense of Washington himself. Monroe led his own reconnaissance mission down the road from Washington to Benedict Creek and sent a personal dispatch to the commander in chief in which he tracked the British, "to take a view of the enemy's movements in this quarter."[21] As the expeditionary force approached Washington on August 24, Monroe briefly joined Madison and his cabinet at the navy yard to try to organize a defense. Realizing little could be done at this late date, he then traveled quickly to Bladensburg to assist General Tobias Stansbury, the commander of the U.S. forces there, in a failed attempt to stop the British march. The appearance of the secretary of state on the battlefield was readily accepted because "Monroe had had as much military experience as other commanders, for none of them was a professional."[22]

Largely because of Armstrong's failure to anticipate the British attack on Washington and his refusal to garrison the city, Madison accepted his resignation and, in early September 1814, made Monroe secretary of war once again, this time on a permanent, not acting, basis. Jealous of his authority, as usual, Monroe wrote Madison on September 3, 1814, stating that he would not assume War Department responsibilities unless the president clarified to one and all that Monroe was the supreme authority at the department.[23] Monroe then directed all his energies to the defense of Baltimore and, organizing support around the military commander General Samuel Smith, helped defeat the British and repel them, finally, from the Chesapeake Bay area. By now, however, the federal treasury was almost bankrupt, and the army was only half its full strength of sixty thousand. "Secretary of War Monroe had been reduced to the expedient of borrowing on a personal basis from state banks to meet the day-to-day needs of his department."[24] In effect, James Monroe was financing the national defense out of his not-too-abundant pocket. Madison, with Monroe's support, was forced to violate Republican principles by endorsing a national bank to finance the war and a conscripted army to fight it. "The Republicans [in Congress] were stunned to learn that the Secretary [Monroe] was abandoning the cherished Republican dogma that the militia constituted the best defense of a free people in order to propose the creation of a conscript army of 100,000 men."[25] Reality trumped ideology. "Our finances are in a deplorable state," he wrote Jefferson at the end of 1814.[26] Monroe did ease Republican consciences by suggesting that it was much more costly to maintain militia forces than regular troops and by refusing to argue that militiamen were less competent fighters. Out of several alternatives, Monroe recommended a recruitment system by which all males between the ages of eighteen and forty-five be formed in groups of one hundred and that each group had the responsibility to keep four men in service at any one time. A substitute measure enabling the states to recruit an army of forty thousand at federal expense was enacted, but the War of 1812 was concluded before it could be put into place.

The negotiation of the Treaty of Ghent ending the war left most

Americans unsympathetic to Monroe's conclusion that the war had unequivocally demonstrated the need for a larger and more effective national defense system.[27] Before departing his post as secretary of war, Monroe prepared a report to the Senate committee on military affairs recommending a peacetime army of twenty thousand, twice its prewar level. He took note of the British army of Canada numbering thirty-five thousand and continuing friction with Spain over Florida and the Louisiana boundaries. He also returned to his familiar theme of the need to increase coastal fortifications, found to be so inadequate during the recent war with the British. Although Monroe privately believed the standing army of twenty thousand to be too small, Congress reduced it by half to its prewar levels. It did, however, appropriate four hundred thousand dollars for a long-term coastal construction program. Monroe thereafter surrendered his War Department post on March 15, 1815.

Almost exactly two years later, on March 4, 1817, President James Monroe delivered his inaugural address in a capital still bearing scars from the flames of war. "The first president to take office since the end of the War of 1812," writes Noble Cunningham, "he commended his countrymen for meeting that test and pictured the nation that had emerged from the struggle as vigorous and flourishing. Dangers from abroad still existed, he cautioned, urging attention to military forces, coastal fortifications, and the state militia."[28] This period would also come to be known, due to the enthusiasm of a Federalist newspaper in Boston in 1817, as "the era of good feelings." As an organized political force, the Federalists were disintegrating, and Jefferson's inaugural claim that "we are all federalists; we are all republicans" had come much nearer to being true. In 1816 Monroe himself had said that "the existence of parties is not necessary to free government."

Partisan battles led by Hamilton and Jefferson had exacted their toll in exhaustion of public patience, and Republicans had sapped Federalist energy and absorbed much of Federalist economic policy by accepting a national bank and a protective tariff by the end of the Madison administration. Monroe's inaugural message acknowledged this mood: "To whatever object we turn our attention . . . we find abundant cause to felicitate ourselves in the excellence of our institutions. During a period fraught with difficulties and marked by very extraordinary events, the United States have flourished beyond example. Their citizens, individually, have been happy and the Nation prosperous."[29] Though the Federalist party might have faded away, individual Federalists and a core set of beliefs did not. And as the historian Gordon Wood notes, the era of good feeling was "filled with bitter factional contention that belied the name people gave the era."[30]

Good feeling or not, Monroe remained focused on national security. "Experiencing the fortune of other nations," Monroe said in his first inaugural address, "the United States may be again involved in war, and it may, in that event be the object of the adverse party to overset our Government, to break our Union and demolish us as a Nation. Our distance from Europe, and the just, moderate, and pacific policy of our Government, may form some security against those dangers, but they ought to be anticipated and guarded against. . . . We must support our rights or lose our character, and with it perhaps our liberties. A people who fail to do it can scarcely be said to hold a place among independent nations. National honor is national property of the highest value. This sentiment in the mind of every citizen is National strength; it ought, therefore, to be cherished."[31]

Concern for the national defense constituted the longest portion of his message. Monroe did not believe the geographic status of the United States as a virtual island nation offered it sufficient security, especially since its maritime interests, seaborne commerce and fisheries, were crucial to its economic well-being. He advocated reform of the state militias, in both training and equipment, and maintenance of a regular army capable of repelling any foreign attack. And, according to one biographer, "he also considered a stronger

defense establishment essential to implement American foreign
policy—a diplomacy based on strength had a far better chance of
realizing its objectives than a policy derived from weakness."[32]

Resurrecting a notion first used by Washington, and no other
president since, Monroe began the first of several planned trips
through regions of the nation. For Washington, the tours were ges-
tures of national unity. Monroe, by contrast, was primarily inter-
ested, writes Noble Cunningham,

> in promoting the nation's military defenses, which he saw as
> implementing the plan enacted by Congress after the War of
> 1812 to construct a chain of fortifications along the coasts,
> bolster defenses on the northern border, and strengthen the
> navy by establishing naval depots and dockyards. His tour
> would not only help him administer the program but also
> build public support for the costly projects. He planned to
> travel north-eastward along the coast and then westward, giv-
> ing particular attention to coastal work, dockyards, forts, and
> other military installations. As acting secretary of war at the
> time of the British burning of Washington in 1814, Monroe
> well remembered the vulnerability of the United States to
> hostile invasion. Building military defenses would become
> one of his major undertakings as president.[33]

The Fourth of July, 1817, found Monroe in Boston, where he cele-
brated the nation's birthday by visiting the famous ship *Independence* and touring Bunker Hill. "It is impossible to approach Bunker
Hill, where the war of the revolution commenced, with so much
honor to the nation," he remarked to a local audience, "without
being deeply affected. The blood spilt here roused the whole American people, and united them in a common cause in defense of their
rights—That union will never be broken."[34] That evening, he was
given dinner by former president John Adams.

By the fall of his first year in office, the border disputes that were
to occupy much of his first presidential term came to the forefront.

A series of lengthy cabinet meetings took place toward the end of October 1817, with much of the time dedicated to thorough discussions of two topics: first, the declarations of independence by new South American republics from Spain, and the proper U.S. response to those new states; and second, the increasing activities by marauding parties operating out of Amelia Island, situated at the mouth of the St. Marys River, between the state of Georgia and the Spanish possession of Florida.

Early on, President Monroe circulated questions and papers to cabinet members prior to meetings, then included the entire cabinet in the lengthy discussions of the matters raised. One such question before this meeting had been: "Is it expedient to break up the establishments at Amelia Island and Galveston [in Texas, within the Louisiana cession], it being evident that they were made for smuggling, if not for piratical purposes, and already perverted to very mischievous purposes to the United States?"[35] After three such cabinet meetings at the end of October 1817, it was decided that the U.S. Army be ordered to disperse the marauders at both Amelia and Galveston. Thus was General Andrew Jackson to enter a stage he had not occupied since his defeat of the British at New Orleans.

On December 2, 1817, President Monroe sent his first annual message to Congress. In it he declared great satisfaction at the rapidly growing national unity and reported that the nation's defenses were "advancing under a well digested system with all the dispatch which so important a work will admit." In the words of Noble Cunningham, "Monroe thus affirmed at the outset of his presidency a strong commitment to the coastal and border defenses of the United States, which his tour earlier in the year had also signaled."[36] He further informed Congress and the American people that he had ordered disruption of the smuggling, slave trading, and pirating at Amelia Island and Galveston.

Following Congress's adjournment on April 20, 1818, Monroe, who had planned a lengthy tour of the southern coast, westward to St. Louis, and returning through Kentucky, instead substituted an inspection of fortifications around Chesapeake Bay, which had featured so large in the War of 1812, and coastal fortification around Norfolk, Virginia. Before leaving, Monroe and his cabinet once again reviewed U.S. policy with regard to revolutions in South America and Andrew Jackson's military operations against pirates and marauders in Florida. The cabinet agreed to order Jackson to remain in Florida at least until Spain could provide proper administration of its possession and to authorize naval patrols to protect American shipping from pirates. Monroe and his secretaries also agreed to "instruct American ministers to declare on their own responsibility that the United States would regard with hostility any interference in Latin America."[37] For his part, Secretary of State John Quincy Adams was unhappy that Monroe was to be absent from Washington for his May tour in the face of what he described as a "rapidly thickening storm" between the United States and Spain over Jackson's military operations in Florida.

Communications were a problem. Events, especially Jacksonian military events, constantly outran the ability to communicate them in a timely manner to Washington. In late April, as Congress adjourned, it was known that Jackson had successfully driven the pirates from Amelia Island. What was not known until Monroe headed from Chesapeake Bay to continue his tour into North Carolina was that Jackson, operating essentially on his own initiative, had summarily executed two British soldiers of fortune, Alexander Arbuthnot and Robert Armbrister, whom he had found guilty of inciting Indian attacks against U.S. citizens, and had continued on from the Spanish establishment at St. Marks (on the Florida panhandle coast south of Tallahassee) to drive the Spanish governor and his garrison out of Pensacola in West Florida. The first action invited war with Great Britain, and the second invited war with Spain. Jackson had become, not for the first or last time, a force unto himself and was unilaterally driving U.S. foreign policy at the point of a sword and not necessarily in a welcome direction.

Returning to Washington, Monroe held a series of cabinet meetings beginning on July 15 to discuss the situation. Led by Secretary of War John C. Calhoun, a majority of cabinet members urged condemnation of Jackson and a thorough investigation into his unauthorized conduct. Alone, and somewhat surprisingly for a secretary of state, Adams strongly endorsed Jackson's initiatives and argued for U.S. retention of both St. Marks and Pensacola. Politics compounded the situation in that Adams, Calhoun, and Secretary of the Treasury William H. Crawford, who supported Calhoun in this critical matter, were all considered competitors to succeed Monroe. Against Adams, the Calhoun majority argued that Jackson had actually carried out acts of war against Spain and, therefore, had usurped the powers of Congress to declare war. For himself, Adams contended that Jackson had acted on the basis of information gathered during his expedition that required further operations against Spanish garrisons in Florida before formal instructions could be obtained from Washington. Monroe used the occasion of a response to the Spanish minister to Washington, Luis de Onis, to pursue an intricate course through the domestic and international political minefields. He eliminated from Adams's draft note any language implying justification of Jackson's behavior and admitted that Jackson had exceeded his instructions but had acted on information gathered while in the theater of combat.

Biographer Harry Ammon concisely summarizes Monroe's behavior and position in this complex affair and offers a valuable insight into his performance as president.

The President, obviously, had long before made up his mind to take a stand short of full endorsement, and had used the Cabinet discussions to reach a consensus midway between the extremes advocated by the Secretaries. With their agreement he could hope to check any movement in Congress to condemn Jackson and thereby cast doubt on his decision to invade Florida. By adopting this position the President also retained the diplomatic advantages gained by the seizure of the posts and avoided the domestic repercussions which might ensue if he repudiated a popular national hero. Moreover, in declining to officially endorse Jackson and by insisting that he had transgressed his orders, the President sidestepped the constitutional issue.[38]

This elegant maneuver did, however, leave Monroe with the unenviable task of communicating to Jackson his reasons for not fully endorsing the latter's military initiatives, which the national hero thought should win universal approval and acclaim.[39] In a letter to Jackson, dated July 19, 1818, Monroe wrote:

> Communicating to you the orders which had been given just before to General [Edmund] Gaines, the views and intentions of the Government were fully disclosed in respect to the operations in Florida. In transcending the limit prescribed by those orders you acted on your own responsibility, on facts and circumstances which were unknown to the Government when the orders were given, many of which, indeed, occurred afterward, and which you thought imposed on you the measure, as an act of patriotism, essential to the honor and interest of your country.[40]

Here Monroe seeks to be clever by simultaneously recording a censure and giving Jackson a script for subsequent justification of his behavior.

In March 1819, demonstrating his continuing concern for security, Monroe undertook yet another tour of fortifications. With Secretary of War Calhoun and his family, as well as a sizable traveling party, Monroe left Washington by steamboat, stopping at Norfolk once again to inspect coastal defenses and surveying sites for what would eventually become Forts Monroe and Calhoun. Monroe continued on to Georgia and then to Nashville, where he spent a week with Andrew Jackson. Monroe shared with Calhoun a great interest in westward expansion and the role military fortifications would play in pacifying that vast region.

As the year 1820 began, the country's thoughts turned to the forthcoming presidential election, and Monroe made no secret of his desire to seek a second term. As it turned out, 1820 was to be "the least-contested presidential race since Washington's unanimous election was decided," in the words of Noble Cunningham.[41] Monroe's reelection was assured when, on the evening of April 8, forty members of the Republican caucus, heeding the call of its presiding officer, Representative Samuel Smith of Maryland, unanimously adopted a motion that it was not expedient to nominate any candidates in opposition to the incumbent president. That same month the Columbus *Ohio Monitor* wrote: "There appears no great excitement in any quarter, concerning the next presidential election. In most of the States the elections occur with great quietness, too great, perhaps, for the general safety of the Republic."[42]

In the fall, only one of the 232 electors, William Plumer, a former Federalist senator who was later then elected governor of New Hampshire as a Republican, cast his vote for John Quincy Adams rather than Monroe. Plumer gave as his reason for dissent his disagreement with Monroe's economic policies and further stated that Monroe "had not that weight of character which his office requires," though Plumer also justified his action by declaring that he wanted no one else to share the great Washington's distinction of having had a unanimous election. But Plumer was decidedly a minority of one. Even former president John Adams, in his capacity as leader of the Massachusetts electors, cast his vote for the incumbent president, despite having once condemned Monroe bitterly for his failures as minister to France.

This virtual unanimity, brought on by the "era of good feelings," was the product of two factors: the first was the collapse of the Federalist party as a political force, though not the disappearance of the Federalist persuasion by any means; and the second was Monroe's conscious efforts to broaden the Republican party's tent beyond the perimeters of its earlier doctrinaire, often dogmatic, ideological orthodoxy. "He now viewed the party as embracing all elements of American society," observes Harry Ammon, "and therefore he accepted the fact that it must also adopt measures meeting the needs of the widest possible spectrum of American opinion."[43]

In this, Monroe was providing a powerful example to future presidents in eras of great change, including Franklin D. Roosevelt, as to how to create a ruling majority that might last a lengthy period of time by adopting policies originally proposed by rival factions. In a later era, it would be said of the Progressives that they got their ideas and rhetoric by waiting for the Populists to go swimming "and then stealing their clothes." Monroe followed a similar tack to gain the support of the former Federalists.

This extraordinary respite of unanimity was not to survive the Monroe presidency. By the election of 1824 and continuing well into the age of Andrew Jackson thereafter, personal rivalries and sectional quarrels erupted to replace the deep philosophical divisions produced by the founding era. Thereafter, those rivalries and divisions would lead to the creation of new factional alignments and eventually new political parties.

Political tensions first began to appear over an issue that Monroe—like many of his successors—would struggle with throughout his years as president: how to balance security and fiscal responsibility, how to match means to ends. In 1819–20, toward the end of Monroe's first term, the nation encountered bad economic times. Monroe himself referred to a "depression in manufactures." Credit contracted, property values plummeted, loan defaults and bankruptcies mounted, exports declined, banks failed. Jefferson wrote to John Adams, "The paper bubble is then burst." This widespread distress led to cuts in the national budget for the next several years. "Most of the cuts were at the expense of the War Department, a branch of the government never popular with old-fashioned Republicans, who looked with horror at the War Department's expenditure of nine million out of a total federal budget of $25.5 million in 1818," writes Ammon.[44]

Within the Monroe cabinet and the Republican party frictions emerged and wounds were opened. Secretary of the Treasury Crawford welcomed the chance to cut the War Department's budget of his presumptive rival for the presidency, Calhoun. Alliances were formed between Crawford allies and conservative (so-called Old) Republicans, joined by the supporters of Congressman Henry Clay of Kentucky, which "virtually wrecked the administration defense program."[45] Monroe and Calhoun had initiated a network of military posts in the Louisiana Territory, much resisted by private trading interests, which wished these lucrative franchises to be privatized for themselves, including a new post on the Yellowstone River. The Yellowstone project "indicated the administration's interest in establishing an American presence near the Canadian border and replacing English traders in the profitable fur trade." Calhoun wrote, "I am very desirous by taking strong and judicious posts to break the British control over the Northern Indians."[46] The beginning of the intense dispute over admission of Missouri into the Union, with its focus on the extension of slavery, would also put much of the reduction of military expenditures in abeyance. Monroe's major interest, the construction and expansion of fortifications, survived with an appropriation of eight hundred thousand dollars, but Congress, in May 1819, required Secretary of War Calhoun to submit a proposal for reduction of the standing army, whose authorized end strength was 12,656 (but whose actual size was 7,421) to 6,000 in order to save an estimated one million dollars per year. Despite these cuts, Calhoun successfully transformed the officer corps and the academy at West Point. According to one Monroe biographer, Calhoun, as a member of Monroe's administration, "was one of the most influential secretaries of war in the nineteenth century."[47]

When Congress reconvened for its 1820–21 session, however, budget deficits were even greater than previously feared and Monroe's fortifications project was cut to $220,000. This greatly distressed the president, who, according to John Quincy Adams, "had set his heart upon its accomplishment, and looks to it as one of the great objects by which his administration may be signalized in the

view of posterity."[48] According to Noble Cunningham, "Congress's
rescission of funding for projects so important to the president was
a humiliating close to his first term, and it did not bode well for the
future."[49] By all accounts, despite James Monroe's almost unanimous reelection in 1820, he had few strong supporters in the new
Congress in his second term. Indeed, in the pithy phrasing of a
letter from Speaker of the House Henry Clay to Adams, "Mr. Monroe has just been re-elected with apparent unanimity, but he has
not the slightest influence in Congress. His career was considered as
closed. There was nothing further to be expected by him or from
him."[50]

Beginning in the fiscal year 1821, the budget cuts in the War
Department began to take effect, and its annual budget fell to just
under five million dollars, where it would remain throughout Monroe's second term. Of the two major military services, the navy survived better because of the useful immediate services it provided in
protecting American commercial shipping from pirates. The strength
of the naval commitment arose in no small part from a congressional decision in President Madison's last year in office to appropriate one million dollars a year for the next eight years for ship
construction, including nine ships of the line, twelve forty-four-gun
frigates, and three steam batteries. This construction took place
largely during Monroe's presidency, even though the naval construction budget was cut in half during the fiscal crisis.

Despite his perceived waning influence and drastic measures by
Congress against military spending, in his second inaugural address,
on March 5, 1821, Monroe once again urged the completion of the
coastal defense program.[51] On matters of defense and national
security, the old soldier was not easily deterred. Further, in the first
annual message to Congress in his second term, in December 1821,
Monroe declared, in a major new initiative, that it had become
"necessary to maintain a naval force in the Pacific for the protection
of the very important interests of our citizens engaged in commerce
and the fisheries in that sea." This led to the establishment, in 1822,

of the Pacific station—"a permanent stationing of naval vessels off the Pacific coast."[52] Further, at Adams's urging, Monroe authorized dispatch of a U.S. frigate to a northern outreach of the Antarctic Peninsula "to strengthen our forces along the American coast" and to frustrate British adventures there. This initiative, it is worth noting, occurred well in advance of the Monroe Doctrine and anticipates Monroe's, and Adams's, definition of U.S. interests as being hemispheric in reach.

The centrality of national security to Monroe's presidency continued throughout his eight years in office and was not deterred by fiscal crisis or waning congressional interest. In his annual message of 1822, he continued his plea for funds for fortifications and managed to secure a five-hundred-thousand-dollar appropriation from the congressional economizers. And in his final message to Congress, on December 7, 1824, announcing a substantial reduction in the national debt, President Monroe repeated yet again his appeal for military posts: "Against foreign danger the policy of the Government seems to be already settled. The events of the late war admonished us to make our maritime frontier impregnable by a well-digested chain of fortifications, and to give efficient protection to our commerce by augmenting our Navy."[53] In his earlier messages he had focused on U.S. relations with Europe and its powers, and on turbulent upheaval in South America, but on this occasion he looked west, as his nation at large was increasingly doing. He requested authorization of a new military post at the mouth of the Columbia River and urged the maintenance of the naval squadron on the Pacific station: "On the Pacific our commerce has much increased, and on that coast, as well as on that sea, the United States have many important interests which require attention and protection."[54] Monroe may not have been the first president to look west, but he certainly was the first to define national security in two-ocean, bicoastal terms.

Historians and biographers have pointed out that there is substantially greater documentation of James Monroe's interest in diplomatic concerns and foreign affairs than in defense and national security matters. However, the same scholars note that much of what we know of Monroe's interests comes from the documents, notes, and diaries of his senior cabinet officers and that, in this respect, the papers and diaries of Secretary of State John Quincy Adams are much more detailed and complete than those of Secretary of War John C. Calhoun. Unlike Calhoun, Adams tended to keep the flurry of notes and scraps of paper Monroe often favored for his communications. "The papers of Secretary of State Adams are filled with memoranda from the president and copies of papers altered and revised by the president or by Adams following his directions," writes Noble Cunningham. He concludes, "Monroe was a 'hands-on' president who devoted himself to his duties and held tightly to the final executive authority," giving closest attention to foreign policy.[55] "Monroe kept well informed about the operations of the War Department, as the inspections of military installations and coastal defenses on his tours of the country illustrated. The president and Secretary of War Calhoun worked closely together during the Seminole war, though he gave Calhoun a freer hand than Adams had in the State Department. Monroe was less immediately involved in financial management than in military matters and foreign affairs."[56] Further, beginning with the Monroe era, it began to be difficult to separate foreign relations from national security.

With the exception of the iconic George Washington, Monroe, among the first half dozen American presidents, is set apart by his consistent lifelong concern for the security of the nation. He was the last veteran of the Revolutionary War to become president of the United States. Though by no means a military hero of the scope of the seventh president, Andrew Jackson, he was a recognized combat veteran before the age of twenty. He witnessed the humiliation of the nation with the burning of the capital in 1814, and did all he could thereafter to prevent any such event in the future. As we shall see, in his search for a more secure nation Monroe would acquire Spanish Florida and complete the southeastern configuration of the

United States. He would, at the same time, extend America's claims westward to the Pacific Ocean and to the Northwest, resisting Russian claims in the process. He would also expand the naval protection of the United States to the Pacific Ocean. He consistently and persistently pursued expansion of fortifications and coastal defenses, placed U.S. garrisons in abandoned British posts in the original Northwest, extended a new network of outposts into the Louisiana Territory he had helped to acquire, and called on Congress, even in dire financial times, to maintain and expand the U.S. Army and Navy.

There was no stronger believer in the principles of the republic than James Monroe. Together with Thomas Jefferson and James Madison, he was a stalwart soldier in the army of the republic. Yet, virtually alone, he broke with Republican orthodoxy in supporting a standing army in peacetime. His experience in Revolutionary combat and in the bitter days of 1814 caused him to put security above ideology. Political and military realities in the classical age of the Greek city-state and early Roman republic might permit reliance on the citizen-soldier, the farmer-warrior. But in the occasionally hostile world of the early nineteenth century, with America still struggling to establish its political and economic institutions, the nation could not rely solely on wide oceans for its protection. Properly trained and equipped regular army and naval forces, under professional, qualified officers, were required to enable an expanding nation to sleep securely at night. Indeed, under Monroe the romantic and highly appealing notion of citizens defending themselves began to be laid to rest. Later, in a twentieth century of world wars and cold wars, professional military forces numbering in the millions would be required for national defense and "power projections." In ways he would not have especially appreciated, Monroe laid the groundwork for that age.

Most memorably, in 1823 he proclaimed principles that positioned the United States as the dominant power in the entire Western Hemisphere. Though a presidential statement of foreign policy principles and not a congressionally endorsed resolution authorizing presidential use of force, the Monroe Doctrine was a foundational statement of the United States' intention to play a wider role in the world.

Following the War of 1812, James Monroe also laid a groundwork for homeland security that would guarantee that no Americans would die on American soil from a foreign attack. That is, until September 11, 2001.

4

James Monroe and
John Quincy Adams

James Monroe's friendships with Thomas Jefferson and James Madison were lifelong and—except for occasional competition with Madison and disappointment with Jefferson over the treaty with Great Britain—enduring. Yet as president, Monroe had no relationship more important than that with his secretary of state, John Quincy Adams.

Geographic distribution weighed heavily in the construction of Monroe's cabinet in advance of his inaugural on March 4, 1817. Ever the dedicated Republican, and constantly aware of ideological differences with the Federalists, Monroe wrote to Andrew Jackson after his election that "the Administration should rest strongly on the republican party." But he also believed he could widen his party's reach by symbolically unifying the nation through widely distributed selection of senior cabinet officers. The office of secretary of state was of special importance because in his case, as well as with Jefferson and Madison, it was generally perceived as a stepping-stone to the presidency. Therefore, his selection would not only heavily influence the direction of his foreign policy, still evolving in the context of an evolving Europe, but also prequalify a probable future president.

Monroe acknowledged this in a letter to Jefferson explaining his choice of Adams: "You know how much has been said to impress a belief, on the country, north & east of this, that the citizens of Virga. [Virginia], holding the Presidency, have made appointments to that dept. [State], to secure the succession, from it, to the Presidency, of the person who happens to be from that State. . . . It is, however, not sufficient that this allegation is unfounded. With this view, I have thought it advisable to select a person for the dept. of State, from the Eastern States, in consequence of which my attention has been turned to Mr. Adams."[1]

John Quincy Adams, son of the second president of the United States who had, in the Federalist movement, been one of Jefferson's polar opposites, had had a distinguished diplomatic career in his own right. His internationalism was ingrained early; at age eleven, he had accompanied his father to Paris. In the last decade of the eighteenth century, while still a young man, he had served in U.S. missions to the Netherlands and Prussia. He had been minister to Russia under James Madison for almost five important years. During that period he had been chairman of the U.S. peace commission at Ghent which had successfully negotiated an end to the War of 1812. Since 1815, Adams had been America's minister to Great Britain. The selection of Adams "assigned a major post to a prominent New Englander of undoubted talents," argues Harry Ammon, one "who possessed unusual diplomatic experience."[2] Perhaps as important to Monroe as this seasoned diplomatic service was Adams's decision to support President Jefferson's controversial 1807 embargo, a highly charged political move that caused him to break with his father's party and join the Republican ranks. In making his selection, Monroe further wrote to Jefferson that he would choose Adams, "who by his age, long experience in our foreign affairs, and adoption into the republican party, seems to have superior pretentions to any there." Added to this considerable diplomatic portfolio was the practical legislative experience Adams had gained as a U.S. senator during Jefferson's second term.

Adams was never to be accused of being physically impressive. One historian described him thus: "Short, fat, bald and plagued with a constantly running eye, he seemed like a pigmy among a race of handsome and vigorous giants." Yet it has been noted that he was genuinely sensitive to the feelings and opinions of others, especially in the intense confines of the cabinet.

In a very brief note dated March 6, 1817, President Monroe wrote to Adams: "Dear Sir, Respect for your talents and patriotic services has induced me to commit to your care, with the sanction of the Senate, the Department of State. I have done this in confidence that it will be agreeable to you to accept it, which I can assure you will be very gratifying to me."[3] It would not be until September 1817 before Adams, then fifty years of age, would conclude his undertakings with the British, move his family back to the United States, and assume his duties at the State Department.

Monroe's principal contact with Adams to this point was during the former's term as secretary of state and the latter's service as U.S. minister to Russia and, in 1815, as minister to Great Britain. Adams's intense activities in negotiating peace with Great Britain following the War of 1812 made him a familiar, seasoned, and sophisticated figure to Monroe. Added to his superior diplomatic experience were the regional balance he offered as an easterner and the balance of "good feeling" he offered as a former Federalist. According to his biographer Robert Remini, the "appointment made a great deal of sense. Who was more qualified than Adams to run the State Department?"[4]

The world John Quincy Adams would seek to relate the United States to was, in many ways, a new one. So much so that, in his magisterial history of the United States during the Jefferson and Madison administrations many years later, Henry Adams, John Quincy Adams's grandson, wrote: "Every serious difficulty which seemed alarming to the people of the Union in 1800 had been removed or had sunk from notice in 1816. With the disappearance of every immediate peril, foreign or domestic, society could devote all its energies, intellectual and physical, to its favorite objects. . . . The continent lay before them, like an uncovered ore-bed."

Not quite. To uncover and develop the ore deposits required both resolution of conflicting boundary claims and security from foreign interference. Both were to preoccupy the Monroe administration for the coming eight years, and both required constant monitoring of and response to new realities, among them the revolutions against Spanish colonialism in South America. But Henry Adams is certainly right in terms of his analysis of the world that confronted Thomas Jefferson in 1800. From the French Revolution, which began a few months into George Washington's first term, to the Treaty of Ghent, concluding the second war with Great Britain in 1814, the United States had been deeply embroiled in European power politics. The War of 1812 had severe economic and political repercussions in the United States and had left the nation's capital in ruins. With the restoration of some political balance after the Congress of Vienna in 1815, as Henry Adams noted, the United States finally had a degree of breathing room it had never had, breathing room to look to domestic expansion and development and to begin the long process of normalizing its relationships with the European powers.

With accelerating westward expansion, with the depression of 1819–20 ending, and with trade among the South (cotton), the West (food and raw materials), and the Northeast (manufactures) expanding, the United States of the second Monroe administration found itself facing a transportation revolution. New York State had undertaken construction of the Erie Canal. Madison had vetoed a bill for federally financed internal improvements, and the congressional authority in this field remained in constitutional doubt. Monroe raised the issue in his first annual message to Congress and believed throughout his administrations that a constitutional amendment was required to authorize Congress to appropriate money for national infrastructure projects. Early in his second term, even though recognizing the need for federal transportation projects, he vetoed a bill authorizing the repair of the interstate Cumberland Road and the collection of tolls, and he did so on the grounds that it exceeded congressional authority under the Constitution. But he was clearly conflicted due to increasing commercial demands and, predictably, because he readily acknowledged the national security requirements for military transport.[5]

Yet, though "Monroe would enter office with Europe and North America at peace," according to Cunningham, "the revolutions in Latin America, together with the presence of Spanish troops in Florida on the southern border of the United States, meant that foreign concerns would return to prominence on the national agenda."[6] This was the backdrop for the first discussion between the new president and his secretary of state in the fall of 1817, a discussion which covered America's relations with Great Britain, whence Adams had just arrived, France, and Spain, but also the growing rebellions in South America. Following this discussion, Adams, constitutionally an activist, initiator, and self-starter, began his practice of peppering his chief with memoranda and what today would be called position papers. Typically, Monroe either edited Adams's language or raised new questions for Adams to clarify. He had already done this with Adams's suggested instructions to Richard Rush, the new minister to Great Britain. A series of early cabinet meetings in late October 1817 focused on the South American revolutions and the rising disturbances on the United States' southern border with Spanish-occupied Florida. Indeed, disturbances in Florida were directly traceable to pirates, smugglers, slave traders, and freebooters emanating from the South American colonies over which Spain was losing control. Amelia Island particularly was being converted, according to Monroe, into "a channel for the illicit introduction of slaves from Africa into the United States, an asylum for fugitive slaves from the neighboring States, and a port for smuggling of every kind."[7] These lengthy cabinet meetings eventuated in orders to General Andrew Jackson to drive the brigands out of Amelia Island and Galveston.

John Quincy Adams's extensive diaries offer valuable insights into Monroe as well as his cabinet throughout his presidency. Among his cabinet colleagues, at least two of whom would become competitors for the presidency, he became closest to John C. Calhoun.

According to Harry Ammon, "a strong and lasting bond was immediately established, for they shared many intellectual interests, a
love of order and logic, and a common enthusiasm for a nationalist
program. . . . It was rather remarkable that these two men of such
disparate background both possessed a puritan conviction of righ-
teousness—for Adams and Calhoun political judgments tended to
be moral rather than pragmatic."[8] At one point early on, Adams
noted of Monroe and his cabinet: "These Cabinet councils open
upon me a new scene and new views of the political world. Here is
a play of passions, opinions, and characters different in many
respects from those in which I have been accustomed heretofore to
move. There is slowness, want of decision, and a spirit of procrastination in the President, which perhaps arises more from his situation than his personal character."[9] This conclusion he derived from
observing Monroe's habit of deferring decisions following cabinet
meetings. Further, Monroe used his extensive cabinet meetings
to develop consensus in his administration. Ammon observes that
"Monroe did not meet with his Cabinet primarily for advice (his
mind was usually already made up on most issues) but to hammer
out an agreement and to secure a commitment to his program."[10]
Adams would comment to himself in his diary regarding Monroe's
slowness, want of decision, and inclination toward procrastination,
but he did not go much further, even in private, in criticizing or
greatly praising his chief. Perhaps most revealing of their friendship
was the mutual warmth and affection that characterized their relationship late in Monroe's life.

The process of politics, however, did not always provide Monroe
the luxury of controlling his response to events. The issue of the
United States' position on the South American republics was being
driven in part by the Speaker of the House, Henry Clay, who,
Adams noted, "had already mounted his South American great
horse" and who was demanding immediate recognition of Buenos
Aires (later Argentina) as an independent republic and support for
other insurrections on the continent. Adams saw this as Clay
maneuvering himself to become the administration's goad and as

positioning himself to run for the presidency to succeed Monroe. Monroe's original policy, "to favor the colonies, to the utmost extent, consistent with the peace, security, and happiness of our own country," was to undergo an evolution over time as he sought to balance instinctive support for republican revolution against colonial oppression against the possibility of a war with Spain brought on by both Jackson's expedition against Florida and U.S. interference in Spanish foreign policy. The balance was also internal to his own government. Clay was the firebrand seeking to plunge the United States into the revolutionary cauldron of South America. Adams, the diplomat, wanted little more than for the United States to declare for principles of liberty and democratic ideals.[11]

Spain's operations in its South American possessions were not admirable. They basically represented trading monopolies and plunder of local resources. As Spain's power had declined in the late eighteenth century, its hold on its colonies in the Western Hemisphere had begun to erode under the influence of commercial freelancers and indigenous patriots drawn toward independence by the American and French Revolutions. It was this latter phenomenon that most attracted support in the United States. As individual colonies declared independence from Spain, they quickly dispatched emissaries to Washington seeking political support, diplomatic recognition, and practical assistance such as trading access to American ports. Because information from that sector of the hemisphere was slow to arrive and unreliable, Monroe dispatched three commissioners on board a U.S. ship of war to cruise the South American coast to assess the political situation firsthand.

Meanwhile, Andrew Jackson, operating on direct orders from Secretary of War Calhoun in December 1817, took command from General Edmund Gaines, who had been conducting operations against renegade Seminoles in southern Georgia. Gaines's prior orders had been to pacify the entire Georgia frontier with Florida and to pursue Seminole and other troublemakers across the border, but to break off engagement with them if they took refuge in a Spanish fortification. Although Jackson took command subject to the same restrictions, for decades it remained in dispute whether he was actually aware of them, particularly since he had previously advocated directly to Monroe that the Spanish fortifications in Florida should be reduced or occupied. The question whether Jackson knowingly exceeded his orders remained an open, and controversial, one for decades to come and up to the very eve of Monroe's death.

For, after driving the marauders and pirates from their redoubt on Amelia Island, Jackson received reports that the Seminoles, complicit in raids on American settlements in southern Georgia, were receiving support from the Spanish garrison farther west at Pensacola, on the Gulf of Mexico. On his own initiative, Jackson attacked and occupied Fort Carlos de Barrancas at Pensacola and deposed its Spanish governor, who promptly fled the wrath of the Hero (Jackson).

This action excited much of the nation and caused a minor uproar in the Monroe cabinet. Secretary of War Calhoun, together with Treasury Secretary Crawford and others, urged the president to repudiate Jackson's activities and restore Pensacola and the fort to the Spanish, arguing, inter alia, that Jackson had violated the Constitution by initiating war without a proper congressional declaration. Adams, for himself alone, argued that Jackson had had broad authorization to terminate Seminole attacks on Americans and that he was merely carrying out orders. Adams wrote in his diary on July 20, 1818, that "the whole conduct of General Jackson was justifiable under his orders, although he certainly had none to take any Spanish fort. My principle is that everything he did was defensive; that as such it was neither war against Spain nor violation of the Constitution."[12] In pursuit of his theory of defensive behavior, Adams had argued before the cabinet

that Jackson took Pensacola only because the Governor threatened to drive him out of the province by force if he did not withdraw; that Jackson was only executing his orders when he received this threat; that he could not withdraw his troops from the province consistently with his orders; and that his only alternative was to prevent the execution of the threat.[13]

Adams's vigorous defense of Jackson might have been more persuasive if Jackson, perhaps unbeknownst to Adams, had not been advocating driving the Spanish out of Florida for years. Indeed, six months before the cabinet debate Jackson had written Monroe directly and confidentially that East Florida should be seized by the United States and that "this can be done without implicating the government. Let it be signified to me through any channel, and in sixty days it will be accomplished." The very prospect of this conquest seemed to cause the Hero to lick his military chops. Reporting directly to President Monroe after this desired mission was accomplished in West Florida as well as East Florida, he wrote: "I have established peace and safety, and hope the government will never yield it, should my acts meet your approbation, it will be a source of great consolation to me, should it be disapproved, I will have this consolation, that I exercised my best exertions and judgment and that sound national policy will dictate holding possession as long as we are a republick."[14] One can almost hear the music of "Old Soldiers Never Die," evoked by an army general of similar character returning from controversial conduct in Korea in the 1950s. Or perhaps Jackson's words are more reminiscent of General George S. Patton. Jackson was essentially saying, "Take it or leave it. It's all the same to me. If you don't like what I did, too bad."

Monroe acted in the matter like a man handed an attractively wrapped present that was ticking loudly. He wrote to Madison that he had three objectives he wished to achieve: to preserve the Constitution (and the congressional prerogative of making war); to eliminate any excuse Spain and its allies might have to declare war on the United States; and, finally, to find a way to turn the entire affair to the advantage of the United States. He addressed the first two by revising a note Adams meant to send to Luis de Onis, the

Spanish minister to the United States, mildly repudiating Jackson's conduct, while trying to explain it in the best light for Jackson, and offering to return the facilities at Pensacola to Spain. To Jackson, Monroe sought to put the best light on a diplomatic nightmare: "The events which have occurred in both the Floridas show the incompetence of Spain to maintain her authority; and the progress of the revolutions in South America will require all her forces there. There is much reason to presume that this act [taking Pensacola] will furnish a strong inducement to Spain to cede the territory, provided we do not wound too deeply her pride by holding it."[15] This step created a friction between Monroe and Jackson, concerning what exactly Monroe intended by ordering Jackson into Florida, that would wax and wane throughout the lifetimes of both men.

Through the entire affair, which would boil and bubble for many months to come, Adams, somewhat miraculously, managed to continue patient negotiations with Spain, through de Onis, for the acquisition of Florida and the definition of the Louisiana Territory's southern and western borders. This despite Adams's description of de Onis as "a finished scholar in the Spanish procrastinating school of diplomacy" and "cold, calculating and wily." Throughout much of 1818, while Adams was negotiating with the Spanish minister, Jackson was busily capturing Spanish posts in Florida. This ability to operate on competing levels may be a tribute to turgid channels of communications. But, as Adams eventually succeeded, Monroe's assessment to Jackson may have had it right. As Adams turned his negotiating beacon on the western definition of Louisiana, Monroe cleverly suggested he seek Jackson's counsel on the matter.

The issue was basically Texas. Popular opinion in the United States favored claiming it, but the Spanish would not hear of it. Adams skillfully got Jackson to agree that acquiring Florida was more important than claiming Texas and that Adams could draw the U.S. boundary at the Sabine River, on the north Texas border. The northern and eastern regions of the United States were jealous of southern and western acquisitions, as they feared these would be used to expand slavery. Brilliantly assessing the domestic implications of this issue, and seeing the Missouri question looming, Monroe counseled Adams to forgo Texas on the correct ground that it would eventually be a matter to settle with a future Mexican government, and because it "involves difficulties of an internal nature [i.e., slavery], which menace the Union itself."[16]

That Adams was fully involved in domestic as well as foreign matters is evidenced by Monroe's discussions with him on such divisive and historic controversies as the admission of Missouri into the Union. The question whether new states entering the Union should or should not be permitted to condone slavery within their borders had been present from the nation's founding. Jefferson, among many others, foresaw the potential awful consequences of the matter but could not frame a resolution. Like a political time bomb, the question awaited a concrete situation requiring national debate and resolution. The application of the Missouri Territory in 1819 to become a recognized state forced the issue and also forced Monroe, a born moderate, into a search for compromise.

Monroe's sentiments in the matter seem more political than moral. In a letter to Jefferson in early 1820, he relates:

> The Missouri question, absorbs by its importance, & the excit'ment it has produc'd, every other & there is little prospect, from present appearances of its being soon settled. The object of those, who have brought it forward was undoubtedly to acquire power, & the expedient well adapted to the end, as it enlisted in their service, the best feelings, of all that portion of our Union, in which slavery does not exist, & who are unacquainted with the condition of their Southern brethren.[17]

Monroe's role in the resolution of the Missouri question has been a matter of continuing controversy, with the majority view being that he refused to exert leadership in its resolution. Unquestionably, he remained behind the scenes. Adams's otherwise meticulous record of the times contains little reference to Monroe until the matter came to a compromise in Congress in 1820. Monroe, abandoning his usual pattern, did not organize a discussion of the matter in the cabinet, undoubtedly to avoid a confrontation between the ardently antislavery Adams and his equally vociferous pro-slavery southern colleagues. There seemed to be little demand from the Congress or the public for a presidential position one way or the other, perhaps because all sides would have presumed Monroe to be aligned with his southern neighbors and original constituents.

Monroe did let it be known privately that he would veto any bill that restricted Missouri's right to determine its own policy on slavery as a condition for admission to the Union. His position was based on what he, and others, perceived to be a constitutional requirement that new states be admitted on the same condition as original states, namely, free to adopt their own policy on this divisive question. Early on, Monroe evidenced more optimism than Adams that a compromise could be found, perhaps because he had learned from his Virginia colleagues that quiet discussions were being held that would extend a line westward from Missouri's southern border (36°30' latitude) above which future states would be free of slavery and below which new states would be authorized to adopt their own policies. When this proposed compromise was formally introduced in the Senate, its supporters began a campaign to get southern senators behind it, and Monroe let it quietly be known that he would sign any legislative measure containing this proposal. This volatile controversy arose one year before Monroe faced reelection. He had more to consider than obtaining support merely in the South. He was president of the entire Republic and, therefore, not at liberty simply to appease his fellow southerners. When his position in favor of the compromise became known in his home state, Virginia's political establishment rose up in revolt.

To his son-in-law, George Hay, a member of the Virginia General Assembly, much in favor of permitting slavery in Missouri and subsequent states, Monroe summarized his position that new states should decide the issue of slavery for themselves. At the same time, in early January 1820, Monroe told Adams that he thought a compromise of the issue was possible. Adams, writing for himself, suspected that an "underplot" was at work in which compromise was being secretly negotiated or "the President has a very inadequate idea of the real state of that controversy, or he assumed an air of tranquility concerning it in which there was more caution than candor, more reserve than sincerity."[18] But Adams apparently still did not understand his chief, for three weeks later Monroe wrote to Jefferson, "I have never known a question so menacing to the tranquility and even the continuance of our Union as the present one [Missouri]." Of a conversation with Henry Clay, leader of the proslavery interests as Speaker of the House and a probable southern competitor of Adams for the presidency, Adams noted in his diary: "[Clay] had not a doubt that within five years from this time the Union would be divided into three distinct confederacies. I did not incline to discuss the subject with him."[19] In early 1818, as Speaker of the House, Henry Clay had introduced the first resolution of statehood for Missouri and had vigorously opposed efforts by antislavery forces to place restrictions on Missouri's admission. But he is widely credited with leadership that led to the Missouri Compromise being adopted by the House on February 26, 1820.

After heated debate within and between both houses of Congress, in March 1820 Monroe was presented with the compromise bills that would admit into the Union Maine, as a state prohibiting slavery, and Missouri, as a state at liberty to set its own policy, including one permitting slavery, and that would prohibit slavery in all other parts of the Louisiana Territory north of the 36°30' parallel. Monroe summoned his cabinet for the first discussion of the issue before signing the bills. He requested cabinet opinions on Congress's authority to prohibit slavery in a territory and on whether the blanket prohibition of slavery beyond Missouri applied only to territories or would continue to be binding on states formed in the Louisiana Territory. All agreed that Congress had the authority to prohibit slavery in a territory, and Adams, an ardent prohibitionist, argued that the authority extended into statehood. There was unanimous agreement that the prospective prohibition was consistent with the Constitution.

Reflecting on all this in his diary thereafter, Adams concluded that his personal support for the Missouri Compromise was sound, "believing it to be all that could be effected under the present Constitution, and from extreme unwillingness to put the Union at hazard." He did, however, speculate as to whether insistence on restrictions against slavery in Missouri might have led to a constitutional convention that would have produced "a new Union of thirteen or fourteen States unpolluted with slavery," which would cause "universal emancipation of their slaves" by all other states.[20]

Monroe had been warned by a number of friends, including his son-in-law Hay, that if he signed a bill prohibiting slavery in new states to be formed in the Louisiana Territory, people in his home state of Virginia and throughout the South would "look out for a new president" in the coming election in the fall of 1820. Those in the North held to the same view if he did not sign the compromise. The ever conflicted Jefferson had been "filled with terror" that the issue might prove "the death knell of the Union. It is hushed for the moment. But this is a reprieve only; not a final sentence."[21]

In the final analysis Monroe based his approval of the Missouri Compromise on constitutional grounds, convinced by his cabinet advisers that nothing in the Constitution prevented such an arrangement, and on the more immediate political grounds that it was the only way in which the Union could be preserved. Justifying his position to Jefferson afterward, he wrote that the Union had been saved "by the patriotic devotion of several members [of Congress] in the slave-owning states, who preferred the sacrifice of themselves at home, to a violation of the obvious principles of the Constitution."[22]

Monroe did not conduct a formal cabinet discussion of the Missouri question until the compromise was about to be approved by Congress in March 1820. Though there is little evidence of discus-

sion between Monroe and Adams, Monroe did recruit Crawford
and Calhoun to collaborate with southern congressional leaders
who were framing the compromise. And Adams, though he wanted
slavery destroyed, "used his influence to persuade his Northern
friends in Congress to accept the compromise."[23]

The Missouri question divided the cabinet, as did many other
controversies of the day. Though the cabinet was Republican in
philosophy, its purposeful geographic breadth virtually guaranteed
regional differences. Further, in Adams, Calhoun, and Crawford,
Monroe had around him three competitors for his succession,
also guaranteeing a degree of competition and tension. Monroe
remained open and neutral to all, summoning cabinet members to
his office with handwritten notes, often on short notice, and wel-
coming visits by them on short notice to him. Monroe invariably
relied on Adams for writing and rewriting those portions of his
annual messages having to do with America's role in the world.
Sometimes Adams would compose and Monroe would edit; at
other times the roles were reversed. There is little if any evidence
that Monroe made statements or decisions regarding foreign affairs
without close consultation with Adams.

Without exception, the issue that most engaged John Quincy
Adams and the Monroe administration was the revolutions sweep-
ing South America during this period. The natural inclination of
U.S. citizens and their leaders was to support the republics emerging from Spanish colonial rule. But few noble causes fail to carry
practical consequences with them, and this cause was no exception.
The temptation to defy Spanish interests in the matter was tem-
pered by the political need to negotiate acquisition of Florida from
Spain and to define the United States' boundary on the southern
and western borders of the Louisiana Purchase. These territorial
interests "dictated a cautious policy—one that expressed sympathy
for revolutionists but maintained a position of neutrality," indeed a
tautological one of "impartial neutrality," in the words of Noble
Cunningham.[24] Giving instructions to the State Department, on
March 24, 1819, Monroe wrote: "The United States has given to

the colonies [in South America] all the advantages of a recognition, without any of its perils." And in a subsequent letter he reiterated this theme: "With respect to the Colonies, the object has been to throw into their scale, in a moral sense, the weight of the United States, without so deep a commitment as to make us a party to the contest. . . . By taking this ground openly and frankly, we acquit ourselves to our own consciences."[25] Under Monroe's guidance, Adams responded to appeals from agents of the South American fledgling republics for recognition and formal relations with assurances of "friendly intercourse" encompassing virtually all the practical advantages, political and commercial, enjoyed by nations with normal diplomatic relations.

In virtually all of his annual messages to Congress, Monroe inserted language sympathetic to the South American causes of liberty. "The revolutionary movement in the Spanish Provinces in this hemisphere attracted the attention and excited the sympathy of our fellow citizens from its commencement," he said in 1822.[26] Adams thought this contrary to a stated policy of neutrality but understood the domestic political considerations of keeping at bay pro-revolutionary congressional firebrands such as Henry Clay. Much of the burden created by the need for tolerable diplomatic relations with Spain was lifted when, on February 22, 1819, Adams, after months of patient negotiations with de Onis, successfully completed the Transcontinental Treaty, which gave the United States possession of Florida all the way to Louisiana and extended the southern boundary of the Louisiana Purchase along a parallel all the way to the Pacific. Of this result, Adams wrote in his diary, "The acquisition of Florida has long been an object of earnest desire to this country. The acknowledgment of a definite line of boundary to the South Sea [Pacific Ocean] forms a great epocha in our history." Adams noted to himself that neither the treaty of independence from Great Britain nor the Louisiana Purchase agreement contained any U.S. claim to a western boundary to the Pacific.

Of the Transcontinental Treaty, finally ratified in 1821, W. P. Cresson writes:

Thus was Jefferson's desire for the Floridas achieved. An acquisition long sought for, essential to internal peace and to preserve the country from the danger of foreign strife and conspiracies, was consummated. For almost twenty-five years, negotiations had been pursued in Spain or Washington, interrupted frequently by periods of suspension of diplomatic intercourse. Europe's internal dissensions, Spain's impotency, and the refusal of England, France, or any other European power to help her had compelled capitulation. The patience, dignity, forbearance, and diplomatic skill of Madison, Monroe, Pinckney, Erving, and Adams had at last achieved the desired end.[27]

This significant expansion to the Southeast and to the West left Monroe free, after the passage of a decent interval, to lay before Congress his intention to grant diplomatic recognition to the South American republics and to request authorization of funds necessary to establish embassies and to normalize relations. It would take Spain two years to ratify the Transcontinental Treaty, and the United States remained cautious so as not to upset this process. Starting in May 1822, all the major South American republics received formal diplomatic recognition by the United States. This historic step would, in turn, lay the groundwork for the even more historic step in 1823.

Adams, though, had not been totally transfixed by Spain and South America. At the beginning of Monroe's second term in 1821, he also closely followed Russian activities along the Pacific Northwest coastal area, including trading posts as far south as San Francisco Bay, as well as British developments in western Canada, extending to claims as far down the Pacific coast as the Oregon Territory. The three nations found themselves territorial and commercial competitors in this vast unsettled region. Concern for South America and the American Pacific in turn had caused Adams to contemplate the notion that "the continents of North and South America were closed to further colonization."[28] It is not clear whether this idea was a notion unique to John Quincy Adams or

whether others, including Monroe, were reaching the same bold
conclusion near the same time. In any case, by 1821, Adams com-
municated to the British minister to the United States, Stratford
Canning, that the United States had no intention of encroaching on
territory in British Canada while Great Britain should "leave the
rest of the continent to us."[29] In September of that year Adams
briskly told the Russian minister in Washington to withdraw settlement claims on the North American continent and, further, that the
United States was adopting the principle that "the American continents [note plural] are no longer subjects for any new European
colonial establishments." This formulation provided a "grandfather"
exception for the British occupation of Canada. With Monroe's
approval, shortly thereafter Adams repeated this assertion to the
Russian minister that, with the exception of Britain in Canada, "the
remainder of both the American continents must henceforth be left
to the management of American hands."[30] Prolonged negotiations
between Washington and St. Petersburg finally resulted in a convention in April 1824 that restricted any Russian establishments
south of 54°40' latitude.

For the Monroe administration and the U.S. government, the
"Americas for the Americans" principle was becoming theological.
In the fall of 1823, Adams boldly stated to the British minister Canning that "the whole system of modern colonialization was an abuse
of government, and it was time that it should come to an end." This
a mere nine years after the army of Canning's nation had burned
the capital of Adams's nation. As Monroe began the preparation of
his annual message to Congress, and thus the nation, in November,
he asked Adams for language on foreign policy to be included in the
message. Adams proposed, "As a principle in which the rights and
interests of the people of the United States are equally involved,
that the American Continents, by the free and independent condition which they have assumed and maintain, are henceforth not to
be considered as subjects for future Colonization by any European
Power."[31]

This bold language substantially outran the capability of the U.S. government to enforce it. There is little if any evidence that thought was given to seeking a congressional resolution authorizing the means to enforce this principle as a policy. During the same period, overtures from the British foreign secretary George Canning, Stratford Canning's cousin, suggested that the government of Great Britain might make naval forces available to prevent the French, on behalf of the Holy Alliance of Russia, Prussia, and Austria, from reasserting Spanish claims in South America, though the British commitment waxed and waned during the fall of 1823. (Essentially a scheme hatched by Czar Alexander I of Russia, the Holy Alliance was meant as a transmonarchical entente based on Christian principles, perhaps an early-nineteenth-century effort to insert "values" into international diplomacy.)

Monroe, as was his regular custom, consulted his two predecessors, Jefferson and Madison, on the subject. Jefferson thought a joint U.S.-British agreement on a "no-European interference in South America" policy was greatly to be desired, especially if Great Britain included itself in the ban.[32]

Monroe and his cabinet sought to reconcile the language to be used in the annual message with similar language to be employed by Adams in his communiqué to the Russian minister in Washington, especially since Russia was a member of the Holy Alliance and the president's message was directed to that alliance as much as to anyone else. Finally, on December 2, 1823, Monroe sent his seventh annual message to Congress, outlining what were to be called then the Principles of 1823 and were later to be referred to as the Monroe Doctrine.[33] The political response in Britain was generally favorable, though George Canning sought to take credit. The czar's court in Russia instructed its minister in Washington to respond to Monroe's message by saying that it deserved "the most profound contempt" but otherwise took no further belligerent steps. For Austria, another alliance member, Count Klemens von Metternich declared privately that Monroe's message represented a "new act of

revolt, more unprovoked, fully as audacious, and no less dangerous"
than the American Revolution. French friends of America, including the Marquis de Lafayette, sent messages of support to Monroe.
That Monroe was heavily influenced by Adams in this matter is
beyond dispute. Adams was an early sponsor, even the creator, of a
"hands-off" doctrine where both the Russians in the Northwest and
the Spanish and the Holy Alliance in South America were concerned. Noble Cunningham, the historian of the Monroe presidency, concludes his analysis of the Monroe-Adams collaboration
on this historic policy in this manner:

> The influence of the secretary of state on the final outcome
> was significant, but it was Monroe who conducted the unre-
> strained cabinet deliberations and drafted—and redrafted—
> his message to Congress until he found a policy that he and
> his cabinet could support. While Adams influenced the content,
> it was Monroe who decided to announce the policy in his mes-
> sage to Congress, thus proclaiming it to the world. . . . In the
> course of time the Monroe Doctrine would become the most
> lasting legacy of the presidency of James Monroe.[34]

Monroe and Adams shared credit for the principles of noncolo-
nization of and noninterference in the New World by European
powers. Adams must be credited with successfully urging the rejection of the British proposal to enforce these principles, though the
British foreign secretary George Canning implicitly withdrew this
offer before it could be accepted. It was Monroe, however, who
rejected Adams's suggestions that the Principles of 1823 be pro-
pounded in diplomatic dispatches and instead announced them to
the world through his widely disseminated message to Congress.
The principal credit for the Monroe Doctrine will continue to be
debated, without clear resolution, between the advocates of Adams
and the advocates of Monroe.

Another Monroe biographer and historian, W. P. Cresson,
reached much the same assessment of the relative roles and rela-

tionship between Monroe and Adams in formulation of the doctrine: "Throughout the long days of discussion Adams played an
undeniably influential and important part, but Monroe was
emphatically the head of the administration, and while he was vigorous and determined to preserve the Western Hemisphere from
European control, he strove to preserve the peace of the world. It
was without a doubt Monroe who thought of dealing with the
Spanish colonial question in his forthcoming message to Congress,
and he who drafted the famous paragraph dealing with the problem."[35] Also noting the tendency to credit Adams with Monroe
administration successes in foreign policy, others have found this
conclusion "far from correct. . . . Monroe, like his predecessors, con-
trolled foreign policy, which was the largest independent authority
vested in the executive."[36]

Beyond the Seminole War, the Louisiana boundary, South American republics, Russia and the Northwest, and the Principles of
1823, a host of other foreign policy matters preoccupied the Monroe presidency and Secretary of State Adams. As with previous
administrations, much time was spent on international commercial
issues, almost all of which were maritime. In Monroe's first term,
Adams sought to promote an international convention regarding
freedom of the seas, which would, inter alia, abolish privateering
and suppress the slave trade. Though the Treaty of Ghent ending
the War of 1812 contained a general condemnation of the practice
of slave trading, to become effective it required authorization of an
international patrol capability to search the ships of all nations, a
measure resisted by Monroe. Monroe and Adams were thus conflicted on the matter: they sought to abolish a practice outlawed in
the United States as early as 1794, but they did not wish to cede
U.S. sovereignty to international authority to do so. In response to
an inquiry by the British minister as to whether there was any
greater evil than slavery, Adams, an ardent antislavery advocate,
responded: "Yes, admitting the right of search by foreign officers of
our own vessels upon the seas in time of peace: for that would be
making slaves of ourselves."[37]

But American public opinion, initially opposed to international inspection and ship searches, was shifting under the influence of an odd coalition of northern abolitionist forces and southern colonializationists, who were pressing for return of American slaves to a new colony in Africa, a colony which came to be called Liberia and whose capital, Monrovia, would be named after the incumbent president. Congressional committees considered legislation granting a limited right of international inspection to suppress slave trading, but Adams remained opposed on the grounds of preservation of national sovereignty. An Anglo-American compromise was sought that would permit open-seas inspections on the grounds that slave trading was a form of piracy and therefore illegal under international laws. This matter having been hanging since the Treaty of Ghent years before, Monroe wanted it dealt with, even over Adams's objections, to clear the way for resolution of a list of British-American disputes including boundaries in Maine and Oregon. In this case, a rare one of fundamental difference between president and secretary of state, the president prevailed over Adams's concern for traditional policy, and, on the piracy theory, the language of the convention on the seas included the compromise permitting limited inspections. Congressional opposition to concession of any right of search turned out to be so great that the proposed convention could be ratified only with an amendment limiting its effectiveness to African coastal waters. Presented with an amended treaty, the British balked and the episode "closed the door permanently on Anglo-American cooperation in suppressing the slave trade." As with other similar initiatives, Monroe's "dream of rapprochement with Great Britain" was sacrificed to domestic politics.[38]

Above and beyond disappointments and disagreements such as this, the names James Monroe and John Quincy Adams would have become historically intertwined inevitably, with or without the famous Monroe Doctrine. Their working relationship was rivaled, at least at this early stage, only by that between Thomas Jefferson and James Madison, lifelong friends and fellow Virginians. Monroe and Adams attained too many historic achievements together over eight years for them to be identified totally separately. They extended America's boundaries south and west. They went far to establish the United States' claim to its continental Northwest. They established the United States as the dominant power in the Western Hemisphere. They vastly increased the United States' position and prestige—whether backed up with concomitant power or not—in the world.

The cornerstone of Monroe's foreign policy, according to Ammon, was to "ensure the recognition of the United States, not only as the strongest power in the Americas, but also as the only one of any consequence in either hemisphere; respect and honor were key words in his thinking."[39] The Monroe presidency was one of the half dozen or so defining presidencies in terms of America's role in the world and its self-definition. The Missouri Compromise, internal improvements, and economic setback and rebound would all require attention. But overwhelmingly, Monroe was required to focus his utmost attention on "whither America" as his nation began to mature into adulthood.

The political man, however, could not be severed from his roots, and his roots in Virginia helped define him and his outlook on his duties. Monroe's connection to Virginia's soil was central to his character. After becoming president, Monroe spent summers outside Washington at Oak Hill, his home in Loudoun County, Virginia, and depended on the regular mails to communicate with members of his administration remaining in or visiting Washington. Originally, Monroe had intended his retirement from the presidency and politics to be spent at the Highlands house in Albemarle. But he soon became more comfortable at Oak Hill, and, being unable to sell it to finance improvements at Albemarle, he settled for continued improvements at Oak Hill. He did not do so gladly, for this represented a more or less permanent separation from his friend and neighbor Thomas Jefferson and other friends in the Albemarle area. The one exception to Monroe's pattern of summering at Oak Hill occurred in the summer of 1823. He remained in the capital until mid-August to review, with Adams, the state of American diplomacy.

The ways in which Monroe himself, his wife, Elizabeth, and their family carried out their social duties as America's first family also help illuminate his complete role as president. Perhaps most impressive in the descriptions of the Monroes as a social couple is the impression made on virtually everyone by Mrs. Monroe. One new congressman wrote to his wife after meeting her at a White House New Year's reception that he found her to be "certainly the finest looking woman I saw" and that she seemed little older than her daughter Eliza, but another foreign visitor commented that she "did not seem especially to enjoy this affair." There were differing views as to the sumptuousness of the Monroe White House table. One congressman found the dinner he attended "dark," perhaps, he wrote, "to hide the nakedness of the President's board." Others found the fare "splendid enough for any Republic." Almost all observers commented on Monroe, in direct contrast with his glamorous wife, as "plain," but also amiable, warm, good-hearted, kind, and courteous. At least one biographer discusses the degree of privacy the Monroes maintained in the White House, scheduling fewer large functions and small dinner parties than their predecessors: "To a remarkable degree, the Monroes lived a completely private life in the White House, enjoying a domestic seclusion respected by their contemporaries, who did not consider the family life of public figures a subject for public curiosity."[40] This may have also been attributable to the fact that many found Elizabeth, as well as her daughter and substitute hostess Eliza Hay, to be formidable women. Though Eliza was considered "vain, proud, and sharp-tongued," the story is told of how she sat up several nights with the Calhouns' dying five-month-old daughter.

As for Elizabeth Monroe, many compared her, naturally but often unfavorably, with her predecessor, Dolley Madison. Mrs. Madison had entertained and exchanged visits so extensively that her health suffered. Mrs. Monroe, of a naturally more fragile constitution, knew her limits and refused to go beyond them regardless of the political consequences. She was already suffering ill health in the White House and was increasingly fragile throughout the remainder of her life. She manages to stimulate, though, the kind of curiosity and interest that would justify further exploration of her as a figure in her own right.

Despite the relative social quiet of the Monroe White House, it was not without a little drama. The story is told of a ministerial dinner at which the British minister Sir Charles Vaughan saw the French minister Count de Serurier, directly across from him, bite his thumb every time Vaughan made a remark. "Do you bite your thumb at me, Sir?" Vaughan finally challenged. "I do," was the Frenchman's reply. They promptly withdrew and were at sword points in an adjoining hall when President Monroe arrived and threw up their swords with his own. Their carriages were called, and Monroe sent them, separately, away.[41]

Later in life, following his departure from the presidency, Monroe spent five years at Oak Hill, where he daily rode his horse and sought to improve his crops through progressive farming methods. The Monroes were once again joined by Eliza and George Hay. Given Elizabeth Monroe's continuing illnesses, Eliza once again became mistress of the house and principal hostess.

Following the examples of his predecessors Jefferson and Madison, Monroe refrained from influencing the policies of the new John Quincy Adams administration. Unlike Monroe with both Jefferson and Madison, Monroe and Adams rarely corresponded and met on only a few occasions after 1825. But they cherished a warm regard for each other. The first time he returned to Washington following his retirement, James Monroe made it a point to call upon his successor and former secretary of state.

5

"This Sets Our Compass":
The Principles of 1823

Early-nineteenth-century Americans were peculiarly sensitive to revolution, a heritage which they understood and with which they had sympathy. Even as they were continuing to sort out relations with their former colonial masters in Great Britain and establishing stable relations with other European powers at the close of the first quarter of the century, revolutions against Spanish colonial rule broke out across South America, including in localities such as Buenos Aires (Argentina), Chile, Colombia, and Mexico. As news of these revolutions spread across the United States, American political opinion became overwhelmingly sympathetic to revolutionary brothers to the south.

The political issue presented to the government of the United States toward the close of James Monroe's second term was whether these revolutionary governments warranted diplomatic recognition, and if so, what impact such recognition might have on U.S. relations with Spain and with Europe in general. America's heart was with the new Latin republics; America's head was with stable, long-term European relations. As Madison's secretary of state, James Monroe led with his heart. He gave serious thought, if not serious advocacy, to recognition of the fledgling republics.

As president, however, Monroe heeded his head, recognizing the need to maintain the tenuous relationship with Spain, at least until troubling matters such as Florida and the boundaries of the Louisiana Purchase were settled. Caution prevailed, and the Monroe policy toward South America was neutrality.[1] Indeed, Monroe approved language, in a draft letter from Secretary of State Adams to the Argentinean agent in Washington in 1818, that summarized the U.S. position to his and other conflicts as "impartial neutrality," an interesting choice of language apparently meant to add a bit of spine to an otherwise less-than-robust policy. But Adams did remind the Argentinean emissary, Manuel de Aquirre, that his infant republic enjoyed virtually all the advantages of recognized nations, including commercial exchange and port access, open communications with the U.S. government, "national hospitality," and "every attention to their representatives which could have been given to the accredited Officers of any Independent Power."[2] Monroe had Adams insert language in this message indicating that he, the president, recognized that Buenos Aires "has afforded strong proof of its ability to maintain its Independence," which would surely "gain strength with the powers of Europe," but that, nevertheless, the United States found it necessary to "move with caution" on the question of full diplomatic recognition.

As cautious as Monroe was, in this instance Adams was even more cautious and consistently more nuanced. Adams thought his chief's insistence on adding this language and in commenting at length in his annual congressional messages on the struggle between Spain and its South American possessions, which he characterized as "civil war," was unnecessary and even counterproductive in that it called into question both the United States' pronounced neutrality and its sincerity. However, Adams also acknowledged the pressure that the Monroe administration was receiving from congressional firebrands, Henry Clay particularly, to publicly avow its wholehearted commitment to the revolutionaries, and concluded that Monroe's "impartial neutrality," though leaning distinctly in the pro-revolutionary direction, had kept his congressional critics at bay.

All this diplomatic and political tightrope walking was occurring against the backdrop of ratification of the Transcontinental Treaty,

signed in 1819. Monroe and Adams rightly believed that concluding the formal acquisition of Florida from Spain and establishing
the United States' claim of the Louisiana boundaries to the Pacific
were of greater importance than recognizing the South American
republics. It was a classic case of a clash between principle and
interest. In the interest of securing southern and western borders,
the principle of solidarity with republican revolutionaries could
wait. Despite Adams's reservations, however, in his 1820 message
to Congress Monroe repeated his declaration of affinity with the
South American republics. And, despite this declaration, Congress
went further and demanded full recognition.

By February 1821, both the United States and Spain had fully
ratified the Transcontinental Treaty, but it was not until more than a
year later that Monroe formally declared a new policy of full recognition of the South American republics and requested congressional authorization of funds necessary to establish embassies and
normal relations. Congress endorsed the new policy with only one
dissenting vote. With presidential pressure, that vote was later
rescinded.

The overarching significance of the struggle over diplomatic
recognition of the new republics was twofold: it set the table for
reconsideration of the perpetuation of colonial systems in the nineteenth century; and it laid the groundwork for redefining America's
larger relationship with Europe and of Europe's relationship to the
Western Hemisphere. Now that U.S. sovereignty over Florida and
the western expanses of the Louisiana Purchase were formally
established, and the United States had officially recognized revolutionary republics to its south, Monroe was at liberty to consider
the broader question whether and how long the European powers
should be able to continue to act out their rivalries on the Western
Hemispheric stage.

To a degree, albeit a lesser degree, the other side of that coin—
the role the United States should play in the affairs of Europe—also
came into question. This was, all in all, a period of serious definition

and redefinition of respective intercontinental rights and roles. And it proved to be a multilayered chess game. Before the Monroe administration recognized the South American republics, Adams received a note from Czar Alexander I's government confirming the Russian monarch's refusal to receive any minister from a new South American country and complimenting Monroe on his neutrality. In this respect Russia was stating the case of the Holy Alliance—Russia, Prussia, and Austria—on behalf of Spain's claims to its South American colonies.

But the Russian intervention in South American issues came at a time of U.S.-Russian friction on relative rights and interests in the still uncertain Northwest. In the fall of 1821, the Russian imperial court issued a decree putting an area within one hundred miles of the Pacific coast north of the fifty-first parallel off-limits to foreign ships. Previous Russian claims had extended southward only to the fifty-fifth parallel. By the summer of 1823 Adams had challenged any Russian rights to territory on the North American continent and first asserted the principle that "the American continents are no longer subject for any new European colonial establishment."[3]

The Holy Alliance had been formed, as much as anything else, as a response to the French Revolution and Bonapartism, to crush any semblance of revolt against the ancient monarchies in Europe. The French army had recently invaded Spain to put down an uprising in Cádiz and, in August 1823, had restored Ferdinand VII as the Spanish monarch. From there, it was a relatively small step to helping secure Spanish possessions in the Western Hemisphere, and the British soon warned the U.S. government that this was in the offing.

Within Monroe's cabinet, Secretary of War Calhoun was credited with agitating the president about European intentions in South America. Not for the first time, Calhoun found himself at opposite ends of an issue from Secretary of State Adams, both of them among the several assumed rivals for succession to Monroe. Adams confided to his diary that "Calhoun is perfectly moon-struck by the surrender of Cadiz, and says the Holy Alliance, with ten thousand men, will restore all Mexico and all South America to the Spanish dominion." But Adams no more believed that the Holy Alliance would undertake such a venture than that "the Chimborazo [an Ecuadorian mountain] will sink beneath the ocean."[4] Whether Calhoun ever came close to being right or not, and there is little evidence that he did, the intentions of Russia and the Holy Alliance added yet another dimension to the diplomatic chess game.

More important in the grand political equation were the interests of Great Britain, possessor of the world's greatest navy, a navy that could most effectively project its power across the Atlantic as was so vividly demonstrated in 1814. The role of Great Britain in the evolution of the Principles of 1823, which defined America's policy in the hemisphere for a century and a half to come, was a complex one. The framework for this role was established in a three-way exchange of diplomatic correspondence first between the British foreign secretary, George Canning, and the U.S. minister to Great Britain, Richard Rush, most of which occurred in a space of days in August of 1823, and then between Rush and Secretary of State John Quincy Adams. Canning opened the bidding on August 19, when, rather offhandedly at the conclusion of a lengthy interview in London with Rush, he asked what response the U.S. government might make to a proposal that Great Britain and the United States exchange commitments to keep France, and presumably the Holy Alliance, from intervening on Spain's behalf to suppress rebellion in the South American colonies. According to Rush's note to Adams regarding the interview, Canning

> asked me what I thought my government would say to going hand in hand with this . . . not as he added that any concert in action under it could become necessary between the two countries, but that the simple fact of our being known to hold the same sentiments would . . . by its moral effect, put down the intention on the part of France, admitting that she should ever entertain it.[5]

Almost before Rush could send his notes of the conversation to his government, Canning memorialized his proposal in writing to Rush the following day. "Is not the moment come when our Governments might understand each other as to the Spanish American Colonies?" he asked. And if such an understanding could be achieved, he continued, "would it not be expedient for ourselves, and beneficial for all the world, that the principles of it should be clearly settled and plainly avowed?"[6] For Great Britain, Canning outlined his government's policy: Spain's desire to recover the colonies was "hopeless"; the independent South American states should be recognized as "time and circumstance" dictated; Great Britain would by no means interfere if the former colonies chose to negotiate their status with Spain; Great Britain had no ambition to possess any portion of them; but transfer of any portion of them to any other power by Spain would not be met with indifference by Great Britain. "If these opinions and feelings are, as I firmly believe them to be, common to your government," Canning concluded, "why should we hesitate mutually to confide them to each other, and to declare them in the face of the world?"[7] From this correspondence, many historians have argued that the notion of the United States defining its principles regarding European intervention in the South American republics originated with the British foreign secretary.

Within three days, Rush responded that the U.S. government most certainly shared the sentiments contained in Canning's note but that his diplomatic instructions did not extend to determining the means or manner for expressing them. By way of preface, he stated: "The government of the United States having, in the most formal manner, acknowledged the independence of the late Spanish provinces in America, desires nothing more anxiously than to see this independence maintained with stability."[8] The same day Rush forwarded Canning's note to Adams with the observation that the "embarrassment" he felt in framing a response that accurately reflected U.S. policy would be alleviated if his answer "receives the President's approbation." In an immediate further exchange of notes, Rush reacted strenuously to Canning's warning that if France successfully restored the South American colonies to Spain, it might seek to convene a congress of great powers in Europe to ratify its deeds. Rush stated that an early British guarantee of the independence of the new republics would greatly accelerate his own government's pursuit of the same policy. A week later Canning responded, resisting any suggestion of an early British commitment to the South American republics.

In mid-October, upon the receipt of the Canning-Rush correspondence of August, Monroe, noting that it involved "interests of the highest importance," sent it for comment and advice to his two immediate predecessors in the presidency, with Madison's copies to be forwarded to him by Jefferson. Monroe acknowledged the "extent and difficulty of the questions" raised by the correspondence and asked for their respective opinions on the "vital" questions they contained. In his transmittal, Monroe gave it as his impression that the United States should "meet" the British proposal and make it known "that we would view an interference on the part of the European powers, and especially an attack on the [South American] Colonies, by them, as an attack on ourselves."[9] He thus raised the bidding from "impartial neutrality" to an extension of U.S. security interests to South America. This formulation—an attack on them is an attack on us—would find its counterpart 139 years later (almost to the day) during the Cuban missile crisis in John Kennedy's public warning that any attack originating from Cuba on any nation in the hemisphere would be considered an attack by the Soviet Union on the United States.

On October 24, Jefferson, in response, wrote: "The question presented by the letters you have sent me, is the most momentous which has been ever offered to my contemplation since that of Independence." He then observed: "That made us a nation. This sets our compass and points the course which we are to steer thro' the ocean of time."[10] Jefferson's letter to Monroe also summarized what came to be known, only many years later, as the Monroe Doctrine: "Our first and fundamental maxim should be never to entangle ourselves in the broils of Europe," an old and persistent Jeffersonian principle, and "our second never to suffer Europe to intermeddle with Cis-Atlantic [Western Hemisphere] affairs."[11] Meanwhile, on October 23, Rush sent a message from London that the British had, "in a most extraordinary manner," withdrawn from the chessboard. After the intense flurry of correspondence, sometimes two notes from Canning in a day, he had heard nothing for over a month and did not intend to "renew the topick" and would "decline going into it again" even if Canning raised it.

The diplomatic question, thus, was quickly migrating from very partial "impartial neutrality" toward the Spanish struggle with its South American colonies, to joint U.S.-British recognition of the independence of the new South American republics, to the possibility of a totally new understanding between the young United States and the much older European powers over their respective spheres of influence. It is difficult to imagine this American diplomatic and political transformation in the absence of the boundary settlements between the United States and Spain over Florida and the western Louisiana boundaries. America's surge of self-awareness and self-definition was founded on the new security it had recently attained from the Transcontinental Treaty of 1819, whose final ratification had taken place only months before. Having defined its continental boundaries, at least until its war with Mexico two decades later, the United States was now presented the opportunity (if not also the necessity) by circumstances in South America to define its hemispheric security interests and to reiterate its lack of interest in the antique European quarrels.

The difference in response between Jefferson and Madison says much about the difference in outlook and political philosophy of the two men, if not also about the difference in the respective relationships between each man and Monroe. As seen from his comments above, Jefferson saw the question presented by the British initiative as epic. "Mr. Jefferson thinks them [the Rush-Canning exchange] more important than anything that has happened since our Revolution," John Quincy Adams confided to his journal.[12] Now that America had won its independence, what role should it play in its hemisphere and, by extension, what role should it play in the world? Since Europe was devolving into "a domicile of despotism," Jefferson told Monroe, America, North and South, should have as its objective to become "a hemisphere of freedom" and should have "a system of her own."[13] Great Britain was the nation that could do us the most harm, he remarked, but by joining us in support of the new South American republics it could also bring us closer together and do us the most good. Having once again disavowed any U.S. interest in Europe, Jefferson then raised the curious question as to whether we had any interest in acquiring a former Spanish province. In answering his own question, he suggested that it would be beneficial to add Cuba as another state in the Union, then added quickly, however, that the price of this acquisition—a war of conquest and alienation of the British—was not worth paying.[14]

For his part, Madison took a more nuanced and somewhat more practical position. From every point of view, he wrote, we must "defeat the meditated crusade" that Canning warned the French had in mind to restore Spain's colonies to that nation. Madison agreed with Jefferson that the British offer presented a win-win situation; America could cement its ties to Great Britain while defeating European ambitions to the south. "It is particularly fortunate that the policy of G Britain tho' guided by calculation different from ours, has presented a co-operation for an object the same as ours. With that co-operation we have nothing to fear from the rest of Europe; and with it the best reliance on success to our just & laudable views."[15] Besides, he reasoned, by allying with Britain the United States could temper Britain's own maritime ambitions. Madison's approach is much more focused on great-power relations, with an overlay of suspicion about British motives, than it is to long-term strategic positioning of the United States. In returning

Monroe's original letter to Jefferson, and forwarding his response to Monroe, Madison joined Jefferson in seeing the South American question as "the great struggle of the Epoch between liberty and despotism" playing itself out in "this hemisphere."[16] It was left to John Quincy Adams to summarize the arguments of the two revolutionary giants in his memoirs: "Mr. Jefferson . . . is for acceding to the [British] proposals with a view to pledging Great Britain against the Holy Allies; though he thinks the Island of Cuba would be a valuable and important acquisition to our Union. Mr. Madison's opinions are less decisively pronounced, and he thinks, as I do, that this movement on the part of Great Britain is impelled more by her interests than by a principle of general liberty."[17]

Great Britain having precipitated the South American issue with the Canning-Rush correspondence, conveyed to the American government through Adams, and Monroe having sought the wisdom of Jefferson and Madison, the stage was now set for both extensive and intensive debate within Monroe's cabinet in November 1823. In addition to the president himself, the principal players were Adams, Calhoun, and other minor cabinet secretaries. The precipitating event was the president's annual message to Congress, to be delivered on December 2. Although, as in the past, the message would be a *tour d'horizon* of domestic concerns, including issues such as internal improvements, Monroe would be required to report to Congress and the American people on the panoply of issues concerning relations with various nations and regions of the world, including perhaps foremost the status of the South American republics. In preparation, Monroe had asked Adams for a memorandum summarizing the range of foreign affairs. Adams, in his response and with particular reference to ongoing negotiations with Russia over conflicting U.S.-Russian interests along the northwest coast, suggested inclusion of the following language: "as a principle in which the rights and interests of the people of the United States are equally involved, that the American Continents, by the free and independent condition which they have assumed and maintain, are henceforth not to be considered as subjects for future Colonization by any European Power."[18]

The first of several cabinet meetings in preparation for the annual message took place on November 7. Whether Minister Rush's October 23 note to Adams revealing the "extraordinary" silence from Canning, had yet arrived in the American capital is unclear, although the nature of the debate suggests that it had not. For a good deal of the discussion concerned whether the United States' position should be unilateral or in collaboration with the British. Calhoun was for collaboration, even if the price were a U.S. commitment not to pursue the acquisition of either Texas or Cuba. Adams demurred, wanting to keep open the possibility that the people of either or both territories might one day seek union with the United States. Monroe was more focused on the main point, raising, perhaps for the first time, the issue of seeming to accept subordination to Great Britain if the United States were to agree to any joint declaration regarding the independence of the South American republics. In this Adams concurred, believing it to be "more candid, as well as more dignified" to notify both the Russians and the French directly and unilaterally of America's resistance to any European intervention in North or South American affairs.

A week later the U.S. government had apparently not received Rush's note, as Monroe—prompted by Calhoun, Adams thought— remained agitated as to how to respond to Canning. Calhoun, Adams thought, still held out the fear of the Holy Alliance intervening in South America on Spain's behalf. Jockeying for position in the 1824 national election was already occurring, with Adams and Calhoun very much on the short list of succession to Monroe and another rival, Secretary of the Treasury Crawford, on the sidelines with what turned out to be a disqualifying stroke. Meanwhile, Rush's dispatches arrived, and Monroe, for one, concluded that Canning's recent silence on a joint declaration meant that the British foreign secretary no longer saw any real danger of a Holy Alliance intervention in South America. At a subsequent cabinet meeting on November 21, Adams informed his colleagues of his intention to deliver a message to the Russian minister to the United States, Baron de Tuyll, to the effect that the United States, while firmly committed to the principles upon which it was founded, had no intention of seeking to propagate them by force or to interfere in the politics of Europe, and in return would expect that "the European powers will equally abstain from the attempt to spread their principles in the American hemisphere, or to subjugate by force any part of these continents to their will."[19]

Monroe then outlined his ideas for his annual message to Congress and made it clear, possibly for the first time, that, quite apart from diplomatic notes to Russia and Great Britain, he intended to present a declaration of principles regarding South America. It had been supposed up to this point that the pesky problems of relations to the new republics and denial of Russian claims to the Northwest were purely diplomatic affairs and therefore to be managed through diplomatic channels. Monroe saw these issues more profoundly and historically, as a unique and timely opportunity for the assertion of U.S. interest and power, a chance for self-definition. Originally, Monroe intended to settle any number of scores, publicly condemning France's invasion of Spain and acknowledging the Greeks' claim to independence from Turkey. In this he had Calhoun's support and Adams's opposition. Not surprisingly, Adams prevailed, and these references were removed in the final message. Perhaps thinking ahead to his own administration which he hoped would come, Adams argued that refusing to pick a fight with the French and the Holy Alliance would guarantee that Monroe's administration would be remembered as "the golden age of this republic."[20]

During a series of cabinet meetings and conferences between Monroe and Adams in the following days, Monroe made an effort to get Adams to conform his diplomatic notes to both Russia and Great Britain to Monroe's own message to Congress, the two occurring almost simultaneously. Consistency in foreign policy nuance was his goal. In pursuit of this consistency, Monroe successfully objected to a proposed paragraph in Adams's draft note that stated America's founding republican principles—one of liberty and dependence on the consent of the governed, and one of independence and resistance to outside imposition of a different form of government from that chosen by the governed.[21] Some critics later saw this as Monroe's "timidity," and others viewed it as a mark of his maturity in refusing to invite a fight with the established European monarchies. Monroe and Adams did agree on a paragraph in the diplomatic notes that conformed to Monroe's message delivered a few days later:

> The United States of America, and their Government, could not see with indifference, the forcible interposition of any European Power, other than Spain, either to restore the dominion of Spain over her emancipated Colonies in America, or to establish Monarchical Governments in those Countries, or to transfer any of the possessions heretofore or yet subject to Spain in the American Hemisphere, to any other European Power.[22]

On December 2, 1823, James Monroe submitted his seventh annual national report to Congress, and it included what were first known as the Principles of 1823 and later as the Monroe Doctrine. His statements were simply a presidential declaration of national principles and never codified in any statute, treaty, or proclamation. Given the importance of the principles, or doctrine, to U.S. diplomatic history, it is worthwhile to read the three paragraphs in which they are contained. The first statement is cast in the context of the ongoing negotiations with Russia.

> At the proposal of the Russian Imperial Government, made through the minister of the Emperor residing here, a full power and instructions have been transmitted to the minister of the United States at St. Petersburg to arrange by ami-

cable negotiation the respective rights and interests of the two nations on the northwest coast of this continent. A similar proposal had been made by His Imperial Majesty to the Government of Great Britain, which has likewise been acceded to. The Government of the United States has been desirous by this friendly proceeding of manifesting the great value which they have invariably attached to the friendship of the Emperor and their solicitude to cultivate the best understanding with his Government. In the discussions to which this interest has given rise and in the arrangements by which they may terminate, *the occasion has been judged proper for asserting, as a principle in which the rights and interests of the United States are involved, that the American continents, by the free and independent condition which they have assumed and maintained, are henceforth not to be considered as subjects for future colonization by any European powers.* (emphasis added)[23]

The second principle was set in the context of America's interest in European affairs, "from which we derive our origin," but it stressed America's steadfast resistance to being drawn into the wars of European nations. Monroe notes the different political systems—monarchy in Europe and a republican form of government in the United States—and concludes:

We owe it . . . to candor and to the amicable relations existing between the United States and those powers to declare that we should consider any attempt on their part to extend their system to any portion of this hemisphere as dangerous to our peace and safety. With the existing colonies or dependencies of any European power we have not interfered and shall not interfere. But with the Governments who have declared their independence and maintain it, and whose independence we have, on great consideration and on just principles, acknowledged, we could not view any interposition for the purpose of oppressing them, or controlling in any other manner their destiny, by any European power in any other light than as the manifestation of an unfriendly disposition toward the United States. In the war between those new Governments and Spain we declared our neutrality at the time of their recognition, and to this we have adhered, and continue to adhere, providing no change shall occur which, in the judgment of the competent authorities of this Government, shall make a corresponding change on the part of The United States indispensable to their security.[24]

Having stated America's principles regarding European interposition in the Western Hemisphere, Monroe then continued to make clear that the United States would pursue its policy of remaining distant from European political affairs.

Our policy with regard to Europe, which was adopted at an early stage of the wars which have so long agitated that quarter of the globe, nevertheless remains the same, which is, not to interfere in the internal concerns of any of its powers; to consider the government de facto as the legitimate government for us; to cultivate friendly relations with it, and to preserve those relations by a frank, firm, and manly policy, meeting in all instances the just claims of every power, submitting to injuries from none. But in regard to those continents circumstances are eminently and conspicuously different. It is impossible that the allied powers should extend their political system to any portion of either continent [North or South America] without endangering our peace and happiness; nor can anyone believe that our southern brethren, if left to themselves, would adopt it of their own accord. It is equally impossible, therefore, that we should behold such interposition in any form with indifference. If we look to the comparative strength and resources of Spain and those new Governments, and their distance from each other, it must be obvious that she can never subdue them. It is still the true policy of the United States to leave the parties to themselves, in the hope that other powers will pursue the same course.[25]

These excerpts from James Monroe's message to Congress yield the following principles:

1. Neither North nor South America should any longer be considered subject to colonization by any European power.

2. Any effort by any European power to extend its monarchical system of government to any portion of the Western Hemisphere will be considered as a hostile act by the United States.

3. Although the United States will not interfere in existing South American colonial relations, any effort to reassert European power over those former colonies who have declared themselves to be independent republics, and have been recognized as such by the United States, will be seen as an unfriendly act by the United States.

4. The United States will remain neutral in any ongoing war between Spain and the new South American republics so long as new circumstances (presumably the intervention of the Holy Alliance) do not require additional steps by the United States to ensure their security.

5. The United States will continue to refrain from interference in the affairs of any European power and will seek to maintain cordial relations with all, but in turn will not itself accept being interfered with by them.

6. Allied European powers (that is, the Holy Alliance) should not seek to impose their monarchical system of government anywhere in the Western Hemisphere. Believing the new South American republics will never be subdued by Spain, the United States will leave those parties to themselves and expects other powers to do the same.

Particular attention is due the fifth principle, which should be called the principle of reciprocity. The conventional, and traditional, understanding of the Monroe Doctrine has almost always been as a unilateralist declaration: Europe is no longer welcome in the Western Hemisphere. In fact, Monroe, and Adams, were stating that the United States also was declaring its policy of noninterference in European affairs, particularly its conflicts. "In the wars of the European powers in matters relating to themselves we have never taken any part," Monroe states, "nor does it comport with our policy to do so."[26] This was consequential in that, as the United States gained maturity, influence, and power, one or another side in the endless European struggles would be seeking alliance with it to add to its side of the scale of influence. Monroe further declared that, aside from South America, "with the existing colonies or dependencies of any European power we have not interfered and shall not interfere."[27] This might provide a degree of comfort to those in Europe who feared America as a militant firebrand with a self-appointed mission to stamp out colonialism, and monarchy, throughout the world. Monroe was saying, according to one historian, it was "only when American rights were menaced that the United States made preparation for defense."[28] What made the difference between the American hemisphere and the rest of the world was the contrast of the two political systems: "It is impossible that the allied powers [European] should extend their political system to any portion of either continent [in the Western Hemisphere] without endangering our peace and happiness," Monroe stated.[29] But he also made it clear the United States had no intention of imposing its political system on any who did not wish it.

Perhaps most significant to America's role in the twenty-first-century world, with its superpower temptations to remake the world in its own image, is this conclusion by Monroe's biographer Harry Ammon: "To Monroe (and his contemporaries) the declaration had only a moral character; it was not an assertion of imperial mission."[30] Here indeed was as clear-cut and comprehensive a statement of U.S. foreign policy as any since the founding of the Republic. These principles defined America's relationship with all Europe, including Great Britain, Spain, and the Holy Alliance. They encompassed the dispute between the United States and Russia over the northwest coast. These principles directly addressed U.S. policy toward the struggle between Spain and its former colonies in South America and warned the Holy Alliance against interposition in that continent. The principles sought friendly relations between all the European powers and the United States and restated an American commitment to remain apart from European politics. Most important, the principles established the entire Western Hemisphere as independent of European dominance. Given the history of the times, Monroe's foreign policy principles were breathtaking in their sweep and comprehensiveness.

Methodologically, they were also important. Monroe chose to decisively separate the entire Western Hemisphere from Europe, thus ending more than three centuries of colonization, not through diplomatic notes and correspondence but by a bold public declaration to the peoples of the world. As Ammon notes, Monroe "focused attention upon his utterances as a declaration of national policy and achieved an impact which was far greater than if the same principles had been embodied in a series of diplomatic notes."[31] From the point of view of domestic politics, Monroe formulated his principles with little, if any, consultation with Congress. His advisory council seems to have been limited to Adams, Calhoun (whom he mostly ignored), one or two minor cabinet members, and Thomas Jefferson and James Madison. And, perhaps most important, Monroe understood the importance of stating these policies independently from the British, further declaring American independence.

Of Monroe's advisers, Adams clearly had the most influence, particularly in that he was also conducting the day-to-day bilateral diplomacy with all the principal nations involved; but even then Monroe prevailed in toning down much of Adams's more confrontational rhetoric. Inevitably, scholars disagree about the degree of credit due Adams for the Monroe Doctrine. For the historian Robert Remini, "it was his [Adams's] statesmanship that led directly

to the formulation of one of the most basic and fundamental pre-
cepts of U.S. foreign policy, namely the Monroe Doctrine. In effect
he established what Samuel Flagg Bemis has called the foundations
of American foreign policy."[32] Other scholars are more inclined to
see the doctrine as the result of a fateful collaboration, and still others give principal credit to Monroe. "The influence of the secretary
of state on the final outcome was significant," according to Noble
Cunningham, "but it was Monroe who conducted the unrestrained
cabinet deliberations and drafted—and redrafted—his message to
Congress until he found a policy that he and his cabinet could support. While Adams influenced the content, it was Monroe who
decided to announce the policy in his message to Congress, thus
proclaiming it to the world."[33]

Monroe sent the text of his congressional message to Jefferson
on December 4 with the following observation: with regard to
South America, "I consider the cause of that country [sic] as essentially our own." In separate correspondence to Jefferson, he justified
his independence from America's former colonial master by asserting that, had the United States joined Great Britain in stating certain of these principles, "it would have been inferr'd that we acted
under her influence, & at her instigation, & thus have lost credit as
well with our Southern neighbors, as with the Allied powers."[34]
Madison, in his response to Monroe's message, concurred in his successor's independent approach: "Whilst the English Govt very naturally endeavors to make us useful to her national objects, it is
incumbent on us to turn . . . the friendly consultations with her, to
ours [national objectives], which besides being national, embrace
the good of mankind everywhere."[35] The ideal of America as both
the beacon and fountain of democracy had been asserted.

Very soon thereafter other American statesmen had occasion to
refer to Monroe's principles in other contexts. In 1825 Henry Clay,
by then Adams's secretary of state, in instructing his envoy to Mexico, Joel Poinsett, reminded him to draw to the attention of the
Mexican government "certain important principles of interconti-

nental law" in reference to U.S.-European relations that were contained in Monroe's message: "The first principle asserted . . . is that the American continents are not henceforth to be considered as subjects to future colonization by any European powers." The other principle was that "whilst we do not desire to interfere in Europe, with the political system of the allied powers, we should regard as dangerous to our peace and safety any attempt on their part to extend their system to any portion of this Hemisphere."[36] Clay apparently thought that the simple declaration of an American president made it law. And a year later, Representative Daniel Webster, in a speech in the House, commented extensively on Monroe's principles that "did great honor to the foresight and the spirit of the [United States] government, and . . . cannot now be taken back, retracted, or annulled, without disgrace."[37]

Speaking today, Monroe might have reduced his foreign policy principles to a single premise: we will resist hegemony without seeking hegemony. Since Monroe's day, however, and with the growth of American political and military power in the late nineteenth and mid-twentieth centuries, what originated as the political principles of a fledgling republic has become a doctrine and subject to imperialistic interpretations.

Monroe's declaration was directly linked to his search for national security through defined borders and political boundaries. He clearly regarded European intervention in South America as a potential threat to the nation's security.[38] Note the benchmarks in his congressional message that had to do with behavior threatening to U.S. security: "our rights and interests," "dangerous to our peace and safety," "indispensable to security," "submitting to injuries from none," and "endangering our peace and happiness." The theme of national security was a consistent one for Monroe. It related to the readiness of the standing forces; the adequacy of coastal fortifications; clearly defined borders and boundaries; and the rejection of European interference in the Western Hemisphere. Monroe went further than any of his four predecessors in linking foreign policy to security.

The degree to which James Monroe's earlier experience as a diplomat, as George Washington's minister to France and as Jefferson's envoy to several European capitals, shaped his foreign policy and the Principles of 1823 is a matter for considerable speculation. During his career as a diplomat, notes Ammon, "Monroe had again and again been humiliated and frustrated by the contempt and indifference manifested by European governments toward the United States."[39] Certainly, in the early days of the Republic, the stature of the United States, and therefore that of its emissary in an important European court, were not the highest. And Monroe's assignment, as that emissary, came early in his career. He never achieved the diplomatic stature of a John Adams, a Benjamin Franklin, or a Thomas Jefferson. He lacked Adams's gravitas, Franklin's charm, and Jefferson's erudition. He was neither worldly nor sophisticated. Particularly where the French were concerned, he surely seemed much more a naif and a rustic, a popular European stereotype and the kind of American found quaint by Old World sophisticates. He went overboard in his enthusiasm for the French revolutionaries and was later mocked by them for it and chastised by his head of state. As a man of limited dimensions, much more the soldier like Washington than the scholar like Jefferson, Monroe saw the world more literally and straightforwardly. Thus he could readily grasp the notion of an old European monarchical world, on the one hand, and a new American republican world in the Western Hemisphere, on the other. He took his republicanism literally and with little nuance. He would intuitively understand a division of the world into two spheres, the world of the past and the world, the American world, of the future. For him, the chance to draw an imaginary line somewhere in the Atlantic would have great appeal. By drawing that line, above all else, America would become more secure.

Monroe very much accepted the Jeffersonian notion that there were two systems of government: monarchical and Old World, republican and New World. The rise of revolutionary republicanism in South America, throwing off the yoke of Spanish tyranny very much as the North American republic had thrown off the yoke of British tyranny, made it possible for the first time to use geography to convert two political systems into two geographic spheres: Western Hemisphere and Europe.

As Jefferson, and Monroe, would not have the United States "entangle" itself in the "broils of Europe," so they would not have Europe cross the Atlantic Ocean to "intermeddle with" American (North and South) affairs. Europe, at least for the time being, would remain monarchical, but the American continents would become a new world dedicated to the restoration of the republican ideal. Jefferson would plant this ideal in the American consciousness rhetorically; Monroe would make it a matter of official national principle.

Arguably, no pronouncement on American foreign policy has had the extended and controversial life that the Monroe Doctrine has had in the more than 180 years since its promulgation. As one historian of the doctrine concluded: "Nothing connected with the foreign policy of the United States has secured and maintained a stronger hold on the popular imagination than the Monroe Doctrine, yet comparatively few know what that 'doctrine' really is."[40]

This sense that Americans consider the Monroe Doctrine to be gospel, yet a gospel with which they are only familiar in passing, is reflected in the observation of Salvador de Madariaga, one of many twentieth-century Latin American observers who have viewed the doctrine not as protection but as a cloak for Yankee suffocation. "I only know two things about the Monroe Doctrine," he observes, "one is that no American I have met knows what it is; the other is that no American I have met will consent to its being tampered with. . . . I conclude that the Monroe Doctrine is not a doctrine but a dogma, . . . not one dogma but two, to wit: the dogma of the infallibility of the American President and the dogma of the immaculate conception of American foreign policy."[41]

Noting that the Monroe Doctrine was neither self-enforcing nor congressionally ratified, the eminent American historian Arthur Schlesinger, Jr., points out that, after an effort by Henry Clay to pass a congressional resolution of endorsement was withdrawn without a vote at the time, no move was made for the next three quarters of a century to place a congressional stamp of approval on the doctrine—that is, until the very end of the nineteenth century, when the Senate, without mentioning the doctrine by name, accepted a reservation to the Hague Convention of 1899 that "implied congressional acceptance of the Doctrine as national policy."[42] "Still," Schlesinger observes, "the Monroe Doctrine, if neither authorized nor ratified, was a notable and unchallenged national commitment." Even so, Schlesinger notes further, there was no basis in the Constitution for Congress or the American people to be under any obligation "to treat improvident presidential declarations as sacred commitments."[43]

It would take the mid-twentieth-century struggle between democracy and communism, as played out in parts of Latin America, to bring the doctrine back to the fore. One historian of the doctrine, Dexter Perkins, wrote in 1955 that "Time and the course of events have altered the scope and perhaps have diminished the relevance of the Monroe Doctrine; but this protean idea is not to be pronounced extinct."[44] As if to prove Perkins's assertion, when the Soviet Union, declaring the Monroe Doctrine to be "dead," warned the United States in 1960 to keep hands off Cuba, the State Department issued a press release stating: "The principles of the Monroe Doctrine are as valid today as they were in 1823 when the Doctrine was proclaimed."[45]

The saliency of the Monroe Doctrine in the twenty-first century is now being tested in a highly convoluted fashion. President George W. Bush's effort to expand the reach of the doctrine globally represents a radical departure from Monroe's original intent in two important ways: first, it extends U.S. hegemony from the Western Hemisphere to the entire globe; and, second, it shifts from U.S. rejection of European colonization in the Western Hemisphere to

U.S. imposition of its values everywhere. Where Monroe sought to protect fledgling South American republics from European intrusion, Bush stands Monroe's doctrine on its head by extending a form of democratic imperialism into the far corners of the planet. James Monroe would be the first to say that America as empire is no longer America as republic.

Conclusion:
The First National Security President

Few would argue that James Monroe was a great president by the standards usually reserved for great presidents. But Monroe has earned the right to be considered a historic, important, and transitional president.

He did not win a great war, though his sure-footed diplomacy with the French, British, and Spanish could well have avoided one. He did not preside over an economic boom, though he did manage to steer out of a significant economic depression. He made no pretension to epic stature, though, in John Quincy Adams, John C. Calhoun, and William Crawford, among others, he surrounded himself with figures of substantial dimensions and was comfortable, and commanding, in their presence. He understood his role on the national political stage was not that of his friends Thomas Jefferson or James Madison, though his presidency was at least as consequential as either of theirs—and arguably more so.

James Monroe seems very much to have been a man attuned to himself. He was, at the core, a public servant ambitious for public office and restless on the political sidelines. He was not above self-promotion, understanding it to be wholly necessary to the achievement of his purposes. But Monroe had a strong sense of self-respect, dignity, and personal honor and would easily take offense, sometimes too easily, with Washington, Jefferson, or Madison when either his motives or his talents were questioned. The strength of his convictions and sense of personal rectitude created personal and political frictions with all those with whom he served. When the adequacy of his performance came into question, his skin could become very thin.

Whether as a young lieutenant at Trenton in 1776, or as secretary of war in 1814, Monroe had an instinct for command. He exhibited initiative when others hesitated, and he had the courage under fire that marks the hero. Though the idea of a purely military career seems not to have seriously occurred to him, Monroe was quintessentially the citizen-soldier. He was of the order of Cincinnatus. He would lay down his plow, law book, or legislative toga and enter the camp of the soldier when the nation was in peril.

Monroe shared with Jefferson and Madison a lack of skill in handling personal financial matters. He could never solve the problem of making his property productive while he was absent serving his country, nor could he generate sufficient wealth to finance his own diplomatic ventures abroad. Thus he was constantly struggling with debt and was preoccupied with financial burdens. He was at his most pathetic when, while desperate to maintain a sense of personal dignity, he found it necessary to petition a series of presidents, secretaries of state, and Congresses for reimbursement of expenses incurred in his nation's service. More often than not his repeated pleas were ignored or denied, often to his abject embarrassment. He borrowed money from family and friends. Even as a retired president, Monroe was petitioning his successors and various Congresses, and awkwardly urging his friends to do likewise on his behalf, for long-denied repayment for service abroad over more than two decades. In a kind of self-imposed internal exile, far from his beloved Virginia home, the fifth president of the United States would die in virtual poverty.

Yet despite these constant burdens and his natural reserve, and despite marriage to a wife who generally sought to preserve her personal privacy, Monroe was a social man who readily accepted the presidential role of public host. Though not a particularly lively man himself, he responded naturally to those who were and seemed to thrive in social settings. Much of the comfort he demonstrated as host seemed to derive from his many years' exposure to diplomatic entertainment in Paris, London, and Madrid. Monroe also demonstrated great pride in his wife and reveled in the extraordinary response her natural beauty and grace evoked.

Conventional wisdom has it that Monroe was a minor star in a Virginia constellation dominated by Washington, Jefferson, and Madison. That was most certainly not how he saw himself, which was as a figure sometimes heavily reliant on Jefferson for philosophical guidance and direction but very much also as a competitor of and equal to Madison, only seven years his senior. Though duly deferential to his immediate presidential predecessor, earlier in his career Monroe had shown no reluctance in disagreeing with Madison over negotiations with the French and the British during the Jefferson administration or competing with Madison for an early congressional nomination or even for the presidency itself. It would be an error of significant proportion to underestimate the strength of James Monroe's streak of independence.

This independent streak can be seen in Monroe's commitment to westward expansion. From very early days he saw himself as a Man of the Western Waters, the title given those who, early on, looked westward and foresaw the nation moving in that direction. At the beginning of his career, and later as president, he traveled to the West. The rights of navigation on the Mississippi for frontier farmers and traders became his continuing concern. The waterways beyond the Allegheny Mountains were, in his understanding, central to western expansion.

Monroe, following Jefferson, believed that western land should be given to Revolutionary War veterans as partial payment of the nation's debt to them. As a principal negotiator of the Louisiana Purchase, Monroe devoted a great deal of energy to the question of access to the Mississippi waterway and to the port of New Orleans for those pushing the frontier westward. From his early days in the Virginia Assembly, where he sought committee assignments having to do with western interests, through his years as president, Monroe, in contrast with the men of the Tidewater plantations and New York and Boston financial centers, was restless to acquire breathing room for the rustic and rough-hewn men looking for freedom and space along the rugged frontier. If America of the early nineteenth century divided itself between the drawing room and the outdoors, between the Jacobs and the Esaus, James Monroe saw himself distinctly among the latter.

Monroe's independence also came into view in his significant departures from republican orthodoxy. Following classical beliefs, those in the Jefferson camp resisted strong centralized government and its attributes, particularly national debt and central banks required to finance that debt and standing armies to protect commercial interests. Central governments borrowed money by issuing bonds guaranteed by national banks. These debt instruments encouraged networks of financial speculators, who, in turn, caused currency fluctuations and economic instability. Nothing good for ordinary citizens could come of it. Savings were devalued and therefore discouraged. Poverty and dependency inevitably ensued. Unrealistic booms and bubbles inevitably led to depressions. Products were then devalued, and labor suffered. Only speculators might gain from highly centralized economies based on private and public debt.

Such economies, for Republicans, went hand in hand with standing armies. Centralized economies created concentrated wealth, which sought foreign markets and commercial advantage abroad. Those in whom wealth was concentrated demanded government protection for their commercial interests and far-flung investments. Such protection could be provided only by professional armies and navies, not militias composed of citizen-soldiers. But every Republican, particularly those imbued with the classics, believed that, from the Greek city-states and the Roman republic onward, standing armies in peacetime were a threat to individual liberties and constitutional republics.

Such was the classical republican orthodoxy of early-nineteenth-century America. This theory, though beautiful, was very much in danger of being murdered by ugly new realities. No new reality was more stark than the British torching of Washington in 1814. Contrary to republican theory, neither the modest standing army nor the state militias could prevent a substantial force of British regulars from having their way with the nation's citadel and seat of government. Despite his heroic efforts, as both secretary of state and secretary of war, to rally the meager troops and protect the capital, Monroe was unsuccessful, and Dolley Madison fled into Virginia with Washington's portrait and the nation's charter.

As president shortly thereafter, Monroe was among the first of his political persuasion to face the new realities of the nineteenth century and understand that a nation that meant to protect itself and make its way in an unstable world of decaying European monarchies would require larger and more professional national security forces. This objective would, alas, require the federal government to be able to pay for these forces, and the only way to do so would be through the creation of a national bank.

For his trouble in addressing forthrightly these new realities, many of Monroe's Republican colleagues and orthodox believers would declare him a heretic and anathema. Yet Monroe saw an America free for the federation of a series of self-governing republics into a union. Primed with the ideals of Aristotle and those of Cato, Cicero, and Livy, the Virginia Republicans feared concentrated wealth and power and the corruption of virtue by interest that inevitably followed. Hamilton's empire of commerce featured greed not duty, financial not popular sovereignty, acceptance of, not resistance to, corruption, and the triumph of special interests over the common good.

No member of the Republican pantheon was more devoted to the classical ideal than James Monroe. A firebrand like Patrick Henry, who would see in George Washington a Caesar or Napoleon, or the rabid John Randolph would outdo him in zeal against the Federalists. Monroe often wrote and spoke of Federalists as alien to the true American culture, parasitical creatures seeking to drain the life's blood from the new Republic. He suspected every motive and doubted every principle of Alexander Hamilton and John Adams, and could accept Adams's son as his secretary of state only because John Quincy had broken with his father's party over the contentious issue of Jefferson's 1807 embargo. When schism rent the Federalists in Monroe's first presidential term, no one could have been more pleased than Monroe. With that, moderate republicanism was finally free to govern America.

But that America was a much different nation than the one founded less than three decades before. It soon contained the Floridas, east and then west to New Orleans, its Louisiana Territory now would extend to the Pacific Ocean, and it laid claim to the Oregon Territory beyond the Columbia River. In this suddenly new America, James Monroe's principal insight was the need for national security, a security that required at the very least a larger standing army, an oceangoing navy, and national fortifications both coastal and inland. And, with the exception of the British firmly entrenched in Canada, it required an entire American hemisphere, north and south, free from European occupation, colonization, and domination.

As Monroe began to see the need for the standing army to double in numbers (but still only modest in size), he, Adams, and other senior cabinet officers evolved foreign policy principles to be contained in his 1823 message to Congress, in diplomatic exchanges, with Russia especially, and in instructions to America's ministers in Europe. These principles were a declaration of the interests of the United States, a definition of its intentions in dealing with other powers, a compilation of guidelines for the conduct of its foreign policy, and a rationalization of America's conduct, all proposed to reduce confusion and establish clarity.

Confusion concerning Monroe's principles—later doctrine—well into the second half of the twentieth century requires an understanding of what they were *not* as well as what they were. These principles were never adopted or ratified by Congress, nor did they contemplate congressional approval, ratification, or oversight. They did not represent a formal treaty between the United States and Great Britain or between the United States and any other European powers. They did not represent an open-ended declaration of war on any foreign nation or power found anywhere in the Western Hemisphere, and therefore could not be invoked, as some would have had it, to authorize military force to drive the Soviet Union out of Cuba in the 1960s and beyond. They were not the early-nineteenth-century version of the 1964 Gulf of Tonkin resolution or the 2002 vote granting authority to invade Iraq. Monroe's principles were, in sum, not self-enforcing.

For those who have wished to employ the Monroe Doctrine as a casus belli, what is often overlooked is the fact that these principles were *reciprocal*. Monroe specifically wanted Spain and the Holy Alliance, or France on its behalf, to cease colonization of South America and wanted Russia to retreat north of the fifty-fourth parallel. Understanding the perils of unilateralism, he also stated the intent of the United States to resist involvement in European affairs. If, as Monroe accurately foresaw, the United States was on its way to becoming a significant force in its own right, one European power or another would seek alliance with the United States against its rival of the day. Monroe, and John Quincy Adams after him, had spent sufficient time in the courts of Europe to appreciate the perils to the Republic in seeking to maneuver through the treacherous shoals, reefs, and sandbars of European political diplomacy. Little good could come of it.

Monroe was sufficiently sophisticated also to know he could not, by pronouncement of *his* foreign policy principles, bind his successors to them. Only as they contained an inner reason and logic relevant to the realities of a changing age could these principles recommend themselves as guidelines for policy in years beyond those in which they were formulated. Who knew—certainly not Monroe—what new and unforeseen forces and factors might lie ahead? Given the central role of John Quincy Adams in formulating these principles, there was every reason to believe that, should he succeed to the presidency (and, in 1823, this was by no means a certainty), he would be guided by them also. But much beyond that, Monroe would clearly understand, his foreign policy principles would be useful and applicable only as they comported with reality.

As to the timing of the announcement of the Principles of 1823, it is important to observe their connection to the conclusion of negotiations with Spain over the extent of the boundaries of the Louisiana Territory. The United States had been under pressure from the South American republics, and their congressional supporters led by Henry Clay, for a number of years for declarations of recognition and diplomatic normalization. Monroe provided them all the advantages of normalized relations without any formal declaration, seeking also not to provide offense to Spain pending completion of the Louisiana negotiations. Meanwhile, Russian expansion southward along the Pacific coastline was requiring some formal declaration of U.S. policy that, at the very least, could not be totally inconsistent with any position the United States might take with regard to other European holdings elsewhere in the hemisphere. After many months of delay, Spanish ratification of the Louisiana treaty permitted promulgation of Monroe's principles, and the annual message to Congress provided the occasion.

Monroe's great insight, one he derived from Jefferson among others, was that the American experiment, possibly now encompassing the entire American hemisphere, was fundamentally different in both its politics and its society from the old orders of Europe and the ancient cultures. This new order required no kings, inherited nobilities, landed oligarchies, masters and servants, or hierarchical social structures and classes. Born in America and accustomed to its boisterous egalitarianism, people like Monroe would witness the vast disparities between the new order and the old during extended diplomatic assignments in European capitals. Monroe could be swept up in the great drama of revolutionary France because, it seemed to him, here lay evidence of a European capability to shed the heavy cloak of monarchy and assume the lighter republican raiment. His enthusiasm would divide him from his more conservative countrymen Washington and John Adams, who, while preferring the new order over the old, nevertheless still favored order over disorder.

As president, James Monroe believed that a unique chance had arisen to quarantine the entire Western Hemisphere from the corrupting influence of European politics. Florida had been added to the territory of the United States. Andrew Jackson had driven the British from New Orleans. The Russians now agreed to stay well north of the Oregon Territory. The western lands, north of Texas and past the Columbia River all the way to the British territory of Canada, were available for expansion. And now, with little need for concern over Spanish diplomatic sensitivities, the new republics of South America could be recognized. For the first time since its Declaration of Independence, the United States had the opportunity to take advantage of its natural oceanic inheritance and assert its hemispheric independence from both autocracy and colonization. Monroe's principles were at once audacious and obvious.

There is little of precedent for twenty-first-century America in Monroe's principles—meant to quarantine republican ideals from monarchical corruption—except for one thing. The world of the twenty-first century is swiftly dividing itself between forces of order and integration and forces of disorder and disintegration. Information, international markets, and travel are bringing participating nations and portions of nations closer together. Religious fundamentalism, tribalism, and ethnic nationalism are elsewhere creating chaos. Both forces are eroding the sovereignty of nation-states.

Whereas no natural boundaries, such as oceans or mountains, can be invoked to separate forces of integration from those of chaos, principles of conduct among nations might help protect the former from the latter. Stable governments can further integrate markets, collectivize intelligence, consolidate security forces, regulate immigration, and prevent state failures. A set of Monrovian principles of today might help create a "western hemisphere" of order, stability, and security separate from another world of instability, disorder, and chaos.

James Monroe could achieve his competing goals of expansion and security because of the alignment of diplomatic stars, the existence of a domestic "era of good feelings" brought on by the decline of Republican-Federalist ideological conflict, and because of the Missouri Compromise. A slave owner from a slave-owning state, Monroe was as conflicted as Jefferson over this national plague, though he agonized less over it. By nature, he was less susceptible to agonizing. But five new states were added to the Union during his presidency, bringing the total to twenty-four. Sooner or later, as states were added north and south of the Missouri Compromise line, great issues of constitutional law and national policy were bound to be raised: Could slavery, as the North wished, be abolished in new states, and, if so, should it be? Or should each new state enter the Union on the same constitutional footing as the original thirteen, that is to say, free to choose for or against slavery for itself? If states were free to choose, would this policy invite a form of land rush in which pro- and antislavery forces competed for domination in settlement? That this latter concern was not totally fanciful is at least partly evidenced by the case of "bleeding Kansas" in the 1850s.

In any case, the application of Missouri for statehood in 1819 brought the matter to an unavoidable front-and-center position. In the search for compromise, Monroe by and large demurred, playing very little part directly and only slightly more of a part indirectly in achieving it. He may claim some role in lumping free-state Maine's statehood application with choice-state Missouri's as a way of achieving northern support for a compromise offering Missouri the right of choice on slavery (with a ban on slavery in future states north of 36°30'). But all eyes were on Monroe throughout the intense congressional negotiations. For if he, a slave-state Virginian, were to veto the compromise, a northern revolt might ensue, and if he were to sign the compromise, the hard-line South, some fellow

Virginians warned, would defect. Despite dire Scylla-Charybdis warnings, sign it he did. And, in so doing, he managed to buy almost four decades of relative harmony for the Union to grow and strengthen before the cancerous matter finally brought secession and civil war.

One of Monroe's biographers speculates that "Monroe probably recalled the controversy over slavery and the admission of Missouri as his most trying crisis," as he reflected on his presidency, "for it had threatened the very existence of the Union."[1] For his part, Jefferson wrote to Monroe that "this is as close as we have come to dissolving our Union since our founding." By helping guide the nation through this treacherous passage, Monroe bought precious time for the Union to gain sufficient stability and resolve to survive the bloody test of its Union.

Like Jefferson, and others to follow, Monroe would step down more than willingly from the presidency when his two terms were completed. "I shall be heartily rejoiced when the term of my service expires," he wrote to Jefferson in words very reminiscent of Jefferson's own, "and I may return home in peace with my family, on whom, and especially Mrs. Monroe, the burdens and cares of my own public service, have borne too heavily."[2] There was broad and contentious competition for his succession in 1824, and Monroe refused to participate or even tacitly suggest a favorite, believing with his predecessors that to do so demeaned the office of the presidency. Yet, somewhat typically of Monrovian politics, the more he stayed aloof, the more his very aloofness was interpreted by one rival as favoring another and the more he was condemned for interference.

Already on the stepping-stone of the Department of State, John Quincy Adams was most likely to succeed Monroe in the presidency. But this was not a fait accompli. In early 1822 one could count as many as sixteen potential contenders for the succession. Adams had the distinct advantage among the lot of being the only New Englander among the half dozen finalists, a group including Crawford and Calhoun from the Monroe cabinet, Speaker of the

House Henry Clay, and General (and now Senator) Andrew Jackson, Adams's eventual successor. "He found himself competing against some of the most engaging personalities in American history." But he was, in the words of one historian, a "cold, austere, and forbidding Puritan," given to "harsh and vindictive judgments" and "cut off from public favor."

The caucus system, whereby candidates were nominated for the presidency by party votes among members of Congress, was under increasing public attack, by Daniel Webster among others, but broader-based party conventions had yet to arise to succeed the caucus. Therefore, the outwardly passive candidate was aggressively promoted by his supporters within the congressional caucus. But those supporters, all being elected representatives, were highly cognizant of the relative popularity of the various candidates in their own states and districts and therefore were not at total liberty to play their own games.

Adams, described by one young foreign observer of the day as "silent and cold" and having "a disagreeable face," was the favorite of New England and much of the North. John C. Calhoun of South Carolina, Monroe's secretary of war and a friend of Adams, was as ambitious as the others but lacked a national following. William Crawford, secretary of the treasury, received the congressional nomination in early 1824 and had a public following but had been incapable of carrying out his public duties due to a concealed illness. Few had been more visible on most issues of national importance in recent years than Clay, described by the same foreign visitor as a "great ladies' man." Unfortunately for Clay, however, the ladies of that day did not have the vote. Then there was Andrew Jackson of Tennessee, war hero and senator, described as having "a charming, open-hearted character, and great elegance of speech." Old Hickory seemed naturally to evoke strong feelings. For some he represented Cincinnatus, the citizen-general, the natural successor to George Washington (and predecessor, perhaps, of Dwight Eisenhower). To others he was a despot-in-waiting on the order of Napoleon (and, perhaps, predecessor of Douglas MacArthur).

After months of colorful combat before open doors, and less seemly combat behind closed doors after no candidate received a majority of electoral votes, on February 9 a series of barter-induced coalitions produced John Quincy Adams as Monroe's successor. Certainly, his relationship to James Monroe and the successes they enjoyed played a large part in his becoming the sixth president of the United States. Like his father, John Quincy Adams turned out to be a marginally successful one-term president. His supporters resented Monroe's neutrality in the contest. Calhoun's and Crawford's supporters resented what they perceived as Monroe's bias toward his secretary of state. Calhoun would settle for vice president and Clay for a very controversial role as secretary of state. Jackson would wait to become president as successor to Adams but would make the intervening years a misery for Monroe by choosing to reopen the sleeping controversy over whether Monroe had, or had not, authorized Jackson's actions in using the Seminole uprisings as an excuse to drive the Spanish out of the Floridas.

This was misery James Monroe did not need, for he would have one of the most unhappy, and undeservedly so, retirements of any American president. For now he was at leisure to contemplate his most immediate, and brutal, reality: debt. Not so much debts he owed others, for he had systematically sold off parcels of land acquired earlier in life to settle his accounts and supplement his modest public salaries, but debts owed him, from his earliest days as Washington's minister to France in 1794, by the government of the United States. He had gone to France to maintain fraternal relations as the United States tacked back and forth between Britain and France. He had returned to France in early 1803, at the urgent request of President Jefferson and Secretary of State Madison first to help negotiate the Louisiana Purchase, then to Spain, and then to London to seek a treaty with Great Britain. Both assignments had required serious financial outlays well above his modest government compensation. And there had always been the expectation, implicit and explicit, that he would be repaid the difference in due course.

Upon returning from France for the first time in 1797, Monroe had submitted his account to Congress for promised reimbursement, but none ever came. Before becoming Madison's secretary of state, he took up with the new president the issue of the costs of his second diplomatic mission and was promised resolution. He refused to pursue the matter while serving for the next fourteen years in the Madison administration and then as president, considering it unseemly. As he approached retirement, neither account had been settled, his lands were depleted, and he had little money with which to support himself.

Humiliation was now required by dire circumstance. He wrote to Jefferson in the final days of his presidency, ostensibly requesting permission to quote from his letter of appointment to France in 1803, to prove the urgency of his departure for his assignment and, therefore, his inability to structure his financial affairs properly. But he may also have been tacitly urging any support Jefferson might offer for his claim. Likewise, he wrote to Madison reminding him of these long-dormant claims and of his intent to submit them once again to Congress.

One happy occasion during Monroe's last month in office occurred with the farewell visit to the United States by Monroe's battlefield friend of some forty-seven years before, the Revolutionary hero the Marquis de Lafayette. Though himself in much the same condition, Monroe used the occasion of Lafayette's visit to lobby Congress to compensate the virtually destitute Frenchman for his service to the United States. The Nation's Guest, as the popular French hero was widely called, was received by official Washington in Congress and by the president at the White House in October 1824. Lafayette joined in the celebration of the anniversary of the surrender of British forces at Yorktown, but the convening of Congress prevented Monroe from participating in a dinner in the rotunda of the University of Virginia at Charlottesville where

Jefferson and Madison honored Lafayette. A notable event occurred at Oak Hill in the summer of 1825, after Monroe's retirement, where for several days he entertained his old acquaintance from Revolutionary War days as well as his presidential successor, John Quincy Adams.

Monroe spent the holiday season of 1824, among his last days in office, rifling through almost three decades of personal papers seeking to compile further documentation of his claims against his own government. In 1826 Congress finally approved a measure providing a portion of Monroe's claims. But for several years thereafter Monroe continued, directly and through friends, to pursue the balance for expenses he thought were owed him. It was a matter of personal pride, he felt, despite the humiliating aspects of his pleas—a matter of simple justice. Almost inevitably, various factions in Congress still supporting Jackson or Calhoun or Crawford took sides opposing Monroe's compensation based not on the merits of his claims but rather on some disagreement over an action Monroe had or had not taken over which they remained angry. Often these were petty disagreements. Years later, toward the end of his life, when Monroe was ill, living in New York with his daughter, dependent on private charity, and for all practical purposes destitute, he finally received a modest payment, sufficient to satisfy most of his remaining creditors but not enough to restore any degree of comfort or dignity.

On top of all this, incredibly, rancor and discord over Jackson's invasion of Florida more than a decade before, over the Missouri Compromise, over internal improvements, and over a wide variety of previous controversies continued to plague Monroe for the remainder of his days. As a man who seemed always primarily concerned with service to his country and to its success and well-being, Monroe's final years were disproportionately sad and undeserved.

After having left office himself, John Quincy Adams passed through Washington in January 1831 and met with Monroe, who was visiting there as well. It was the first time in American history when two former presidents were in the nation's capital at the same time. Adams found his predecessor strikingly emaciated. For a long time the congenitally strong Monroe had been wracked by a cough, possibly undiagnosed pneumonia, that kept him bedridden for periods of time. But, until his last year when his horse fell on him at Oak Hill, Monroe managed to ride every day.

Family tragedy plagued his last months. And troubles came not in single spies but in battalions. In the spring and summer of 1830, his son-in-law and close adviser George Hay became extremely ill and sought relief in the warm springs to the South. His wife and Monroe's daughter Eliza had to attend her granddaughter's birth in Baltimore and, thus, was unable to be with her husband, who, at death's door, sought to return to her and died at Albemarle on the way. Eliza was returning to Oak Hill with her husband's body when Monroe's wife, Elizabeth, fell desperately ill and, shortly after Eliza's arrival at Oak Hill, died on September 23.

Prostrate at his life partner's death, Monroe had to be taken to New York to be looked after by his younger daughter, Maria. In one of his last letters, James Monroe recounted his loss to a friend whose wife had also recently died: "We have both suffered, the most afflicting calamity that can befall us in this life, and which, if time may alleviate it, it cannot efface. After having lived, with the partner of your [illegible], in so many vicissitudes of life, so long together, and afforded each other comforts which no other person on earth could do . . . to have her snatched from us, is an affliction which none but those who feel it, can justly estimate."[3] Thereafter, he was forced to sell the Loudoun County property, which had been his summer home while president. He was now virtually destitute and increasingly reclusive. Indeed, most New Yorkers did not know the former president was resident in their city.

In his later years, Monroe had especially treasured a letter upon his retirement from the presidency from his boyhood schoolmate and neighbor John Marshall, the longtime chief justice of the United States. "In the momentous and then unlooked for events which have since taken place," Marshall wrote, "you have filled a large space in the public mind, and have been conspicuously instrumental in

effecting objects of great interest to our common country. Believe
me when I congratulate you on the circumstances under which
your political course terminates, and that I feel sincere pleasure in
the persuasion that your administration may be viewed with real
approval by our wisest statesmen."[4]

After serving in Monroe's cabinet and succeeding him, John
Quincy Adams remained friendly and loyal. In his inaugural
address, Adams had paid tribute to his chief with as good a sum-
mary of James Monroe's historic achievements as exists anywhere.

> There behold him for a term of eight years, strengthening
> his country for defense by a system of combined fortifications,
> military and naval, sustaining her rights, her dignity and honor
> abroad; soothing her dissentions, and conciliating her acer-
> bities at home; controlling by a firm though peaceful policy
> the hostile spirit of the European Alliance against Republican
> South America; extortion by the mild compulsion of reason,
> the shores of the Pacific from the stipulated acknowledgment
> of Spain; and leading back the imperial autocrat of the North,
> to his lawful boundaries, from his hastily asserted dominion
> over the Southern Ocean. Thus strengthening and consolidat-
> ing the federative edifice of his country's Union, till he was
> entitled to say, like Augustus Caesar of his imperial city, that
> he had found her built of brick and left her constructed of
> marble.[5]

Few claimed for Monroe what he never claimed for himself,
namely, a superior intellect. Especially in the company of a Jefferson or a Madison, he would not shine. His mind was orderly and
logical, moving methodically from evidence to conclusion. His
writings are largely devoid of the classical Greek and Roman references and allusions so predominant in the prose of Jefferson and
others of the Founders. John C. Calhoun perhaps best described the
workings of Monroe's mind: "Tho' not brilliant, few men were his

equal in wisdom, firmness and devotion to his country. He had a wonderful intellectual patience, and could above all men, that I ever knew, when called on to decide an important point, hold the subject immovably fixed under his attention, until he had mastered it in all of its relations. It was mainly to this admirable quality that he owed his highly accurate judgment. I have known many much more rapid in reaching a conclusion, but few with a certainty so unerring."[6]

Wisdom, intensity of focus, and sound judgment, then, were the hallmarks of his mind and character. Even more brilliant leaders might wish for these. Such qualities suited James Monroe's times exceedingly well. The United States was leaving adolescence and entering youthful maturity. Founding ideologies—federalism and republicanism—were blurring, cracking, and merging under the pressure of circumstance and new realities. Additional land for growth and expansion was required. By negotiation and conquest, new borders were being defined. The toxic issue of slavery had to be kept caged as the Union added states. Manufactures began to replace agriculture as the dominant national economic engine. The westward movement demanded an Indian resettlement policy. The slave trade had to be curbed. Internal improvements, especially roads and canals crossing state boundaries, would eventually have to become federal undertakings. Perhaps most of all, European colonial activities in the Western Hemisphere would have to end. In an emerging and uncertain world, the United States would require a much greater sense of national security, the ability to define its legitimate economic, political, and geographical interests and to defend them.

Not every national political figure of the day could have read the compass accurately and have guided the ship of state surely in these rapidly shifting currents. But, despite little evidence of genius, James Monroe managed to do so. For his efforts he deserves higher marks in the nation's formative years than those he is traditionally given.

As a nineteen-year-old Virginia lieutenant charging the Hessian guns at Trenton in 1776, nearly at the cost of his life, he exhibited the unswerving sense of duty, courage, and honor that would characterize his life. He was the last—and second of only two—veteran of the Revolutionary War to serve as president of the United States.

James Monroe died five years to the day after his friend and mentor Thomas Jefferson. The date was July 4, 1831.

Notes

INTRODUCTION

1. W. P. Cresson, *James Monroe* (Chapel Hill: University of North Carolina Press, 1946), p. 28. This entire story was told, according to Cresson, by President Monroe to Lewis S. Coryell of New Hope, Pennsylvania, at a White House dinner.
2. Ibid., p. 14.
3. Ibid., p. 21.
4. Ibid., p. 24, n. 14.
5. Ibid., p. 25.
6. Ibid., p. 51, n. 11.

1: THE PORTRAIT OF A PATRIOT

1. Harry Ammon, *James Monroe: The Quest for National Identity* (Charlottesville: University of Virginia Press, 1990), p. 28.
2. Ibid., p. 30.
3. Cresson, *Monroe*, p. 70, n. 18.
4. Ibid., p. 72.
5. James Monroe to Thomas Jefferson, November 1, 1784, *The Political Writings of James Monroe*, ed. James P. Lucier (Washington, D.C.: Regnery, 2001), pp. 38–40. Hereinafter cited as *Political Writings*.
6. Cresson, *Monroe*, pp. 79–80.
7. James Monroe to Patrick Henry, *Political Writings*, pp. 31–33.
8. Ammon, *Monroe*, p. 43
9. Cresson, *Monroe*, p. 82.
10. Ammon, *Monroe*, p. 60.
11. Ibid., p. 62
12. Ibid.

13. Cresson, *Monroe*, p. 95.
14. Ammon, *Monroe*, p. 69.
15. See the author's *The Minuteman* (New York: Free Press, 1997).
16. Ammon, *Monroe*, p. 76.
17. Ibid., p. 77.
18. Ibid., p. 79.
19. Ibid., p. 81.
20. Ibid., p. 84, n. 15.
21. Noble Cunningham, Jr., *The Presidency of James Monroe* (Lawrence: University Press of Kansas, 1996), p. 21.
22. Ibid., p. 87, n. 25.

2: WASHINGTON'S LIEUTENANT, JEFFERSON'S PUPPET, OR MADISON'S PAWN?

1. Joyce Appleby, *Thomas Jefferson* (New York: Times Books, 2003), pp. 32–33.
2. Carl J. Richards, *The Founders and the Classics* (Cambridge, Mass.: Harvard University Press, 1994), pp. 107, 112, 140.
3. *Political Writings*, p. 256.
4. Ammon, *Monroe*, p. 112, n. 17.
5. Cresson, *Monroe*, pp. 124–25.
6. Richard Brookhiser, *The Founding Father* (New York: Free Press, 1996), p. 83.
7. Ammon, *Monroe*, p. 112.
8. Cunningham, *The Presidency*, p. 4, n. 10.
9. Ibid., n. 11.
10. Ibid., p. 114.
11. Ibid., n. 31.
12. Cresson, *Monroe*, p. 128, n. 4.
13. Cunningham, *The Presidency*, p. 5.
14. Cresson, *Monroe*, pp. 128–29.
15. Ibid., p. 131.
16. *Political Writings*, pp. 111–13.
17. Ammon, *Monroe*, p. 122.
18. Ibid., p. 148.
19. *The Oxford Companion to United States History*, ed. Paul S. Boyer (New York: Oxford University Press, 2001), p. 403.
20. Cresson, *Monroe*, p. 140, n. 14.
21. Brookhiser, *Founding Father*, p. 83.
22. Quoted in Ammon, *Monroe*, p. 155.
23. Cresson, *Monroe*, p. 154, n. 26.
24. Ammon, *Monroe*, p. 129, n. 75.
25. Quoted in ibid., p. 168.
26. Quoted in Cresson, *Monroe*, p. 209.
27. Ammon, *Monroe*, p. 164.
28. Quoted in ibid., p. 177.

29. Thomas Jefferson to James Madison, January 13, 1803, *Jefferson's Works*, iv., p. 453, cited in Henry Adams, *History of the United States during the Administrations of Thomas Jefferson* (New York: Library of America, 1986), p. 292.
30. Ibid., p. 469.
31. Ibid., p. 468.
32. Ibid., p. 717.
33. Ibid., p. 878.
34. Ibid., p. 1015.
35. Ammon, *Monroe*, p. 268.
36. Ibid., p. 278.
37. Ibid., p. 287.
38. Quoted in Cresson, *Monroe*, pp. 247–48.
39. Ammon, *Monroe*, p. 382.
40. Ibid., p. 29.
41. Garry Wills, *James Madison* (New York: Times Books, 2002), p. 91.
42. James Monroe to James Madison, March 23, 1811, *Political Writings*, p. 435.
43. Ammon, *Monroe*, p. 313.
44. Ibid., pp. 312–14; also see, Wills, *James Madison*, p. 117.
45. Cresson, *Monroe*, p. 259.
46. Ibid., p. 273.
47. Ibid.
48. Ammon, *Monroe*, p. 341.
49. Ibid., pp. 352–54.

3: "WE CANNOT GO BACK"

1. Ammon, *Monroe*, p. 44.
2. Ibid.
3. Thomas Jefferson to James Monroe, November 24, 1801, quoted in Anthony F. C. Wallace, *Jefferson and the Indians* (Cambridge, Mass.: Harvard University Press, 1999), p. 17.
4. Ammon, *Monroe*, p. 46.
5. Cunningham, *The Presidency*, p. 2.
6. Quoted in Cresson, *Monroe*, p. 71, n. 25.
7. Ibid., p. 79.
8. Ibid.
9. Cunningham, *The Presidency*, p. 39.
10. "To Congress—Removal of Indians," *Political Writings*, pp. 324–27.
11. Ammon, *Monroe*, p. 91.
12. Ibid., p. 177.
13. Ibid., p. 345, n. 1.
14. Quoted in Ammon, *Monroe*, p. 193.
15. Ibid.
16. Ibid., p. 315.
17. Ibid., p. 323.

18. "Explanatory Observations: Defense of the Coast," *Political Writings*, pp. 448–59.
19. James Monroe to James Madison, *Political Writings*, pp. 462–63.
20. "To the President," *Political Writings*, p. 464.
21. Ibid., p. 333.
22. Ammon, *Monroe*, p. 333.
23. Ibid., p. 337.
24. Ibid., p. 338. See also Cresson, *Monroe*, p. 275.
25. Ammon, *Monroe*, p. 557.
26. James Monroe to Thomas Jefferson, December 21, 1814, *Political Writings*, pp. 470–72.
27. Ammon, *Monroe*, p. 345.
28. Cunningham, *The Presidency*, p. 29.
29. First inaugural address, *Political Writings*, pp. 487–95.
30. Gordon S. Wood, *The Radicalism of the American Revolution* (New York: Alfred A. Knopf, 1991), p. 298.
31. First inaugural address.
32. Quoted in Ammon, *Monroe*, p. 370.
33. Cunningham, *The Presidency*, pp. 30–31.
34. Ibid., p. 37.
35. "To the Members of the Cabinet," *Political Writings*, p. 499.
36. Cunningham, *The Presidency*, p. 43.
37. Ibid., 45, n. 14.
38. Ammon, *Monroe*, p. 420.
39. The entire episode of Jackson's invasion of Florida is discussed at greater length in chapter 5.
40. James Monroe to General Andrew Jackson, *Political Writings*, pp. 502–6.
41. Cunningham, *The Presidency*, p. 106.
42. Quoted in Lynn W. Turner, "Elections of 1816 and 1820," in Arthur M. Schlesinger, Jr., and Fred L. Israel, eds., *History of American Presidential Elections, 1789–1968*, 4 vols. (New York: McGraw-Hill, 1971), 1:316; cited in Cunningham, *The Presidency*.
43. Ammon, *Monroe*, p. 366.
44. Ibid., p. 470. The War Department's expenditure was more than 35 percent of the federal budget.
45. Ibid.
46. Quoted in Cunningham, *The Presidency*, pp. 75–76.
47. Ibid., pp. 110–11.
48. Quoted in Ammon, *Monroe*, p. 471, n. 21.
49. Cunningham, *The Presidency*, p. 112.
50. Quoted in Ammon, *Monroe*, p. 472, n. 26.
51. Second inaugural address, *Political Writings*, pp. 526–35.
52. Cunningham, *The Presidency*, p. 119.
53. Eighth annual message to Congress, *Political Writings*, pp. 541–44.
54. Quoted in Cunningham, *The Presidency*, p. 172, n. 42.
55. Ibid., p. 118.
56. Ibid.

4: JAMES MONROE AND JOHN QUINCY ADAMS

1. Quoted in Cresson, *Monroe*, p. 291.
2. Ammon, *Monroe*, p. 361, n. 51.
3. James Monroe to John Quincy Adams, *Political Writings*, p. 494.
4. Robert V. Remini, *John Quincy Adams* (New York: Times Books, 2002), p. 48.
5. *Political Writings*, pp. 549–602.
6. Cunningham, *The Presidency*, p. 23.
7. Quoted in Cresson, *Monroe*, p. 299, n. 53.
8. Ammon, *Monroe*, p. 359.
9. Quoted in Cresson, *Monroe*, p. 292, n. 39.
10. Ammon, *Monroe*, p. 384.
11. Ibid., p. 446.
12. Quoted in Remini, *John Quincy Adams*, p. 55.
13. Cresson, *Monroe*, pp. 312–13, n. 35.
14. Quoted in Cunningham, *The Presidency*, p. 60, n. 23.
15. Quoted in Cresson, *Monroe*, p. 316, n. 41.
16. Quoted in ibid., p. 325.
17. James Monroe to Thomas Jefferson, February 7, 1820, *Political Writings*, pp. 516–17.
18. Quoted in Cunningham, *The Presidency*, p. 97, n. 29.
19. Quoted in Cresson, *Monroe*, p. 345, n. 8.
20. Quoted in Cunningham, *The Presidency*, p. 104, n. 56.
21. Quoted in ibid.
22. Quoted in Cresson, *Monroe*, p. 458, n. 28.
23. Ammon, *Monroe*, pp. 450–51.
24. Cunningham, *The Presidency*, p. 149.
25. "Sketch of Instructions for Agent for South America," *Political Writings*, pp. 611–16.
26. Message to Congress, March 8, 1822, *Political Writings*, pp. 616–19.
27. Quoted in Cresson, *Monroe*, p. 326.
28. Ammon, *Monroe*, pp. 481–82.
29. Quoted in Cresson, *Monroe*, p. 413.
30. Quoted in Cunningham, *The Presidency*, pp. 149–63.
31. Quoted in ibid.
32. James Monroe to Thomas Jefferson, October 17, 1823, Thomas Jefferson to James Madison, October 24, 1823, *Political Writings*, pp. 632–37.
33. Seventh annual message to Congress, *Political Writings*, pp. 637–51.
34. Cunningham, *The Presidency*, p. 151.
35. Cresson, *Monroe*, p. 439.
36. Ammon, *Monroe*, p. 362.
37. Quoted in ibid., p. 521.
38. Ibid., p. 527.
39. Ibid., p. 409.
40. Ammon, *Monroe*, p. 405.
41. Cresson, *Monroe*, pp. 364–65.

5: "THIS SETS OUR COMPASS"

1. Cunningham, *The Presidency*, p. 149.
2. Quoted in ibid., p. 150, n. 2.
3. Quoted in ibid., pp. 151–52, n. 10.
4. Quoted in ibid., p. 155, n. 2.
5. *Political Writings*, pp. 621–24.
6. Ibid., p. 623.
7. Ibid., p. 624.
8. Ibid., p. 625.
9. Ibid., p. 632.
10. Ibid., p. 633.
11. Thomas Jefferson to James Monroe, *Political Writings*, p. 632.
12. From the memoirs of John Quincy Adams, *Political Writings*, p. 637.
13. *Political Writings*, p. 632.
14. Ibid.
15. James Madison to James Monroe, October 30, 1823, *Political Writings*, p. 635.
16. Ibid., p. 637.
17. From the memoirs of John Quincy Adams, November 15, 1823, *Political Writings*, p. 637.
18. Quoted in Cunningham, *The Presidency*, p. 156, n. 30.
19. Quoted in ibid., p. 156, n. 34.
20. Quoted in ibid., p. 158.
21. Ibid., p. 159, n. 44. This later came to be known as the "no transfer" principle and had first been asserted by Congress in 1811 with reference to Spanish ownership of East Florida.
22. *Political Writings*, p. 640.
23. Ibid., p. 649.
24. Ibid., p. 650.
25. Ibid.
26. Ibid.
27. Quoted in Cunningham, *The Presidency*, p. 160.
28. Ibid.
29. *Political Writings*, p. 650.
30. Ammon, *Monroe*, p. 491.
31. Ibid., p. 492.
32. Remini, *John Quincy Adams*, p. 51.
33. Cunningham, *The Presidency*, p. 163.
34. James Monroe to Thomas Jefferson, *Political Writings*, pp. 651ff.
35. James Madison to James Monroe, *Political Writings*, pp. 653–54.
36. Ibid., pp. 654–55.
37. *Political Writings*, pp. 655–58.
38. Ammon, *Monroe*, p. 479.
39. Ibid., p. 491.
40. David Y. Thomas, *One Hundred Years of the Monroe Doctrine, 1823–1923* (New York: Macmillan, 1923), p. vii.

41. Salvador de Madariaga, *Latin America Between the Eagle and the Bear* (New York: Praeger, 1962); quoted as an epigraph in Donald Marquand Dozer, *The Monroe Doctrine: Its Modern Significance* (New York: Alfred A. Knopf, 1965).
42. Arthur Schlesinger, Jr., *The Imperial Presidency* (Boston: Houghton Mifflin, 1973), p. 27.
43. Ibid., p. 316.
44. Dexter Perkins, *A History of the Monroe Doctrine* (originally published as *Hands Off: A History of the Monroe Doctrine*) (London: Longmans, 1955), p. 393.
45. Cited in Dozer, *The Monroe Doctrine*, p. 186.

CONCLUSION

1. Cunningham, *The Presidency*, p. 191.
2. Quoted in ibid., p. 172, n. 41.
3. Quoted in Ammon, *Monroe*, p. 569, n. 75.
4. Quoted in ibid., p. 468.
5. Quoted in ibid., p. 469, n. 1.
6. Quoted in Cresson, *Monroe*, p. 369.

Milestones

1758 Born April 28 in Westmoreland County, Virginia
1774 Admitted to the College of William and Mary, Williamsburg, Virginia
1776 Declaration of Independence signed; Monroe enlists as a cadet, Third Virginia Regiment
1778 Takes officer's oath for the Continental army
1782 Elected to House of Delegates, Virginia Assembly; later that year, elected to Executive Council, Virginia Assembly
1783 Elected to Confederation Congress
1786 Marries Elizabeth Kortright of New York
1787 Northwest Ordinance enacted by Confederation Congress, with Monroe as one of its leading proponents; Constitutional Convention meets in Philadelphia to draft U.S. Constitution
1788 Elected a delegate to the Virginia ratifying convention
1789 George Washington elected president of the United States
1790 Elected U.S. senator from Virginia
1791 Bill of Rights ratified
1794 Appointed minister to France; Jay Treaty signed
1796 Monroe recalled from his post as minister to France; John Adams elected president of the United States
1800 Thomas Jefferson elected president of the United States; Monroe becomes governor of Virginia

1803 Appointed envoy to France to negotiate Louisiana Purchase; later that year, appointed minister to Great Britain

1805 Travels to Madrid to bid for claim to Florida territories without success

1806 Called on by John Randolph to return to the United States and challenge Madison in bid for presidency but declines; successfully negotiates treaty with British to resolve maritime and commercial conflicts, but it is rejected by Jefferson

1808 James Madison elected president of the United States

1810 Elected to Virginia House of Delegates

1811 Elected governor of Virginia; shortly thereafter, appointed secretary of state by President Madison

1812 United States declares war on Great Britain

1814 Appointed acting secretary of war; British invade and burn Washington, D.C.; Treaty of Ghent signed in December to end War of 1812

1816 Elected president of the United States

1818 U.S. troops, commanded by Andrew Jackson, invade Florida, seizing Spanish military posts and attempting to drive the Spanish governor out of Pensacola

1819 Transcontinental Treaty (Adams-Onis Treaty) signed with Spain, ceding territory of the greater Florida area to the United States and establishing the southwestern border of the United States

1820 Reelected president of the United States; House adopts Missouri Compromise allowing Missouri to set its own policy on slavery but barring slavery north of 36°30' latitude

1822 Establishes Pacific station for permanent stationing of naval vessels along the Pacific coast

1823 Announces the Principles of 1823, later known as the Monroe Doctrine

1825 Retires to Oak Hill, Loudoun County, Virginia

1831 Dies July 4 in New York City

Sources

Among the sources used in this work are the following:

ORIGINAL SOURCES

Appleby, Joyce, and Terence Ball, eds. *Jefferson: Political Writings.* Cambridge: Cambridge University Press, 1999.

Brown, Stuart Gerry, ed. *The Autobiography of James Monroe.* Syracuse, N.Y.: Syracuse University Press, 1958.

Lucier, James P., ed. *The Political Writings of James Monroe.* Washington, D.C., Regnery, 2001. (An invaluable compilation that contains all the important public documents, correspondence, and other papers of James Monroe's life and presidency.)

Richardson, James D., ed. *A Compilation of the Messages and Papers of the Presidents, 1789–1907.* Vol. 2, *James Monroe.* Washington, D.C.: Bureau of National Literature and Art, 1908.

BIOGRAPHIES OF JAMES MONROE

Ammon, Harry. *James Monroe: The Quest for National Identity.* Charlottesville: University of Virginia Press, 1990. (A recognized scholar in early American history and foreign policy provides a full-scale biography, the most recent, and an especially thorough explication of Monroe's foreign policy.)

Cresson, W. P. *James Monroe.* Chapel Hill: University of North Carolina Press, 1946. (A biography that is focused as much on Monroe the man as Monroe the president. The author, a diplomat and lecturer, is particularly effective in his descriptions of Monroe's private life.)

Cunningham, Noble, Jr. *The Presidency of James Monroe.* Lawrence: University Press of Kansas, 1996. (The best modern account of the Monroe presidency, unrivaled as a scholarly treatment of the man and his presidency.)

Gerson, Noel. *James Monroe: Hero of American Diplomacy.* New York: Prentice-Hall, 1969. (A popular treatment meant for younger and general readerships.)
Gilman, Daniel Coit. *James Monroe.* Boston: Chelsea House, 1983. (Another popular treatment suitable for younger and general readers.)
Wilmerding, Lucius, Jr. *James Monroe: Public Claimant.* New Brunswick, N.J.: Rutgers University Press, 1960.

RELATED BIOGRAPHIES

Appleby, Joyce. *Thomas Jefferson.* New York: Times Books, 2003.
Remini, Robert V. *John Quincy Adams.* New York: Times Books, 2002.
Wills, Garry. *James Madison.* New York: Times Books, 2002.

HISTORIES

Achenbach, Joel. *The Grand Idea: George Washington's Potomac and the Rise of the West.* New York: Simon & Schuster, 2004.
Banning, Lance. *The Jeffersonian Persuasion: Evolution of a Party Ideology,* Ithaca, N.Y.: Cornell University Press, 1978.
Bemis, Samuel Flagg. *John Quincy Adams and the Foundations of American Foreign Policy.* New York: Alfred A. Knopf, 1950.
Dangerfield, George. *The Era of Good Feelings.* London: Methuen, 1933.
Fischer, David Hackett. *Washington's Crossing.* New York: Oxford University Press, 2004.
Gaddis, John Lewis. *Surprise, Security, and the American Experience.* Cambridge, Mass.: Harvard University Press, 2004.
May, Ernest R. *The Making of the Monroe Doctrine.* Cambridge, Mass.: Harvard University Press, 1975.
McCoy, Drew R. *The Elusive Republic: Political Economy in Jeffersonian America.* Chapel Hill: University of North Carolina Press, 1980.
Perkins, Dexter. *A History of the Monroe Doctrine.* Originally published as *Hands Off: A History of the Monroe Doctrine.* London: Longmans, 1955.
Peterson, Merrill D. *The Jefferson Image in the American Mind.* Charlottesville: University Press of Virginia, 1998.
Richards, Carl J. *The Founders and the Classics.* Cambridge, Mass.: Harvard University Press, 1994.
Rosenfeld, Richard N. *American Aurora: A Democratic-Republican Returns.* New York: St. Martin's Press, 1997.
Sellers, M. N. S. *American Republicanism.* New York: New York University Press, 1994.
Sisson, Daniel. *The American Revolution of 1800.* New York: Alfred A. Knopf, 1974.
Wallace, Anthony F. C. *Jefferson and the Indians.* Cambridge, Mass.: Harvard University Press, 1999.
Wood, Gordon S. *The Radicalism of the American Revolution.* New York: Alfred A. Knopf, 1991.

Acknowledgments

I would like to express special appreciation for and thanks to Paul Golob, with whom it has been my pleasure to work on this and other books, for his erudition in history, among many other fields, his keen and knowing editorial eye, and the subtle and skillful way he has of setting errant authors back on the proper course. He added at least as much as the author to an understanding of James Monroe's presidency and was more a colleague than an editor on this project. Every author should be so fortunate.

I am also indebted to the eminent American historian Professor Joyce Appleby both for her suggestions of sources for this book but perhaps even more so for the great scholarship she has provided for us on our nation's founding era.

Index

ABOUT THE AUTHOR

GARY HART represented Colorado in the U.S. Senate from 1975 to 1987. He is the author of fourteen books, including most recently *The Fourth Power: A Grand Strategy for the United States in the Twenty-First Century*. Hart has lectured at Yale University, the University of California, and Oxford University, where he earned a doctor of philosophy degree in politics. He recently completed a three-year assignment as cochair of the U.S. Commission on National Security for the 21st Century and is currently senior counsel to the multinational law firm Coudert Brothers. He resides with his family in Kittredge, Colorado.